W9-AXC-368

I
Never Forget
a Meal

AN INDULGENT

REMINISCENCE

I
Never Forget
a Meal

AN INDULGENT

REMINISCENCE

MICHAEL
TUCKER

LITTLE, BROWN AND COMPANY
Boston New York Toronto London

First Edition

Library of Congress Cataloging-in-Publication Data
Tucker, Michael.
   I never forget a meal / Michael Tucker. — 1st ed.
     p.   cm.
   ISBN 0-316-85625-8
   1. Cookery. 2. Food. 3. Tucker, Michael. I. Title.
TX714.T83   1995
641.5 — dc20   94-45970

10 9 8 7 6 5 4 3 2 1
MV-NY
Published simultaneously in Canada by Little, Brown & Company
(Canada) Limited

Printed in the United States of America

For Jill

Contents

Acknowledgments

This book was urged through its many stages by a number of loving specialists and I would like to take this opportunity to thank them. Jane Dystel and Miriam Goderich of Jane Dystel Literary Management were the first to encourage my foray into the writing business and were my first literary critics. I want to thank them for being gentle. Jennifer Josephy was and is the most empathetic and nurturing editor a fellow could find. She also knows how to say no. I thank her for her good taste. Peggy Freudenthal and DeAnna Lunden handled the mammoth copyediting chores. I thank them for their persistence.

Alison Tucker helped me in many ways: typing, computer lessons, elements of style, and, most important, recipe testing. She is a fine cook in her own right, an organized person, and a loving and supportive daughter.

Kim Sterton and Kelli Lawlor did the recipe testing along with Alison and myself. They have worked for the Tuckerberrys for years — in the kitchen and the office — and are indispensable. I taught them how to cook and they can now sauté rings around me.

And finally, I thank Jill, for listening to every page as it came out and giving me her honest opinion. It's not easy being honest — not in love or literary criticism — and the fact that I have someone who I know will tell me the truth, tempered with love, has made writing this book a joy from beginning to end.

I
Never Forget
a Meal

AN INDULGENT

REMINISCENCE

Introduction

When I was in acting school back in the early sixties, I learned
an exercise called sense memory. I would close my eyes and try
to recall an event in my life that carried a big emotional pay-
load — like an argument between my parents or the death of
someone close to me. As I tried to imagine myself back in that
moment, the teacher would ask, "What can you feel between
your fingers? What smells are in the room? What sounds can
you hear — even the ones in the background?" If I could be
very specific about all the sensory input, an amazing thing
would happen. Rather than remembering the emotion, I would
actually feel it — exactly the way I felt it all those years ago.
The same tears would spring to my eyes; the same tingle of fear
would creep up the back of my neck.

The stories in this book are memories, each one prodded
back to life by the sensual evocation of the meal I was tucking
into at the time. Why food? Because the prospect of a good
meal — whether I am cooking it, eating it, or just talking about
it — has always stirred my senses. When I was a kid, a trip to a

restaurant was always the most exciting excursion — more than a movie, or the circus, or even a ball game. Maybe this was because my mom was always on her best behavior there. Under the scrutiny of waiters, she doted on my dad as if he were the duke of Windsor; in front of the well-dressed customers, she beamed with calm beneficence at my brother and me, the perfect progeny in our smartly tailored outfits. In a fine restaurant, my family seemed to sit in a golden circle of light. This was not always true of the meals we had at home.

Perhaps I am obsessed by food because cooking was one of the earliest outlets for my creativity. When I was a little kid waiting for my parents to come home from a party, I perfected the grilled cheese sandwich. I played with different colors, textures, and tastes. I mixed Swiss with Gorgonzola or port-wine Cheddar with Monterey Jack. I was an artist, flying on inspiration. I experimented with techniques like sautéeing the sandwich in butter while pressing down on it with a heavy plate to ooze the ingredients together and crisp the texture of the bread. I developed audacious flavor combinations, like adding mustard and dill pickle to Cheddar on dark pumpernickel before grilling. Never mind that all these things had been done by others before; in my mind they were innovations. In my imagination I was a genius.

As I got older, food took on a symbolic significance as well as being a source of pleasure. A good meal reminds me that I am alive and that life is good. My wife might argue that sex, not food, provides that feeling for me, but I would assert that they are one and the same thing. Of course, I'm talking about really good food.

So, in looking back at my life from the age of fifty or so, the names and faces fade into obscurity, dates and events tumble confusedly into one another, and yet I can remember with perfect clarity whether it was rosemary or thyme on the roast chicken in that little bistro in the Dordogne some thirty years ago. The food is my touchstone; it piques my taste buds, which, in turn, prod my memory. This book is a look at my life through food, a medley of my greatest meals — triumphs and fiascoes — parading before my eyes like the visions a drowning man might have while going under for the third time in a large vat of chicken stock.

ONE

A Child's Crab Feast
in Baltimore

When I was nine or ten years old, we went for a long
weekend down to Middle River in east Baltimore — my mom,
my dad, my brother, and I — to visit the Haases, Lil and Phil. It
wasn't my first trip to their place nor my last, but it's the one
that will stick forever in my memory. Lil worked for my dad in
the fur department of the Hochschild-Kohn department store
in downtown Baltimore. My dad was the buyer and Lil was his
crackerjack salesperson. They had worked together for what
seemed all my life. Her husband, Phil, whom I knew less
well — from Christmas parties and the like — worked for
Bethlehem Steel and did something that required him to wear a
metal hat. What struck me then and always about them was that
they were the only blue-collar friends my parents had — gentile blue-collar to boot — and visiting them always felt a little
as if we were going to a foreign country and maybe we should
get shots or something. Both my father's and mother's families
were insular. They tended to be comfortable only within their
very close-knit family units. I think this was typical among first-

7

generation immigrant families. Brothers and sisters were each other's best friends, and it was rare that an outsider broke through. If that sounds limiting in terms of numbers, it should be noted that my mother was one of seven children and my father one of fifteen. Add in spouses and offspring and they had quite a variety to pick from. There were even enough people around within the family circle for them to find someone they chose not to speak to. My mom and dad were even mistrustful of each other's families — the Prosers and the Tuckers tended to eye each other warily when they were brought together for major holidays or celebrations. My father thought all the Prosers were crazy and my mom thought the Tuckers were narrow-minded. And as I look back on it, they were both right. Weddings or bar mitzvahs tended to break down by the end of the evening into a Lithuanian version of the Hatfields and the McCoys.

But the Haases managed to break through. The simple charity of their personalities was undeniable. And they were fun. They were easy with each other and with us; they loosened up my parents like no one else could. They loved to joke and tease, to eat and drink, to laugh about our differences — ethnic, economic, and religious. I remember them still as among the best people I've ever known.

They had a ramshackle house, or cabin really, on an estuary of Chesapeake Bay. It was just a big eat-in kitchen with a fireplace and a series of sleeping porches, some of which had been enclosed, some just screened in. I guess there was a bathroom somewhere, but I can't recall. The whole thing seemed like it was going to blow down any minute. And there was a dock — also barely standing — to fish or swim from.

We arrived at around noon, and the steamy August heat was already above the ninety-degree mark. My mom and dad sat out on rusty metal lawn chairs and had a drink with Lil. They watched as Phil prepared to take my brother, Ed, and me out in the boat to check the crab pots. He had a string of them stretched out into the bay, and we would motor up to them, one at a time, to empty the day's catch. Phil had on an old red-and-black-checked flannel shirt and an even older pair of jeans, which in those days we called dungarees. I remember that when he bent over the side of the boat to check the lines, they revealed more of Phil's posterior than Ed or I ever expected to see. We, on the other hand, were wearing what my mother deemed proper clothing for a visit to the shore — matching pants and shirt ensembles that would be called leisure suits at a later time. Phil looked at us with a mixture of wide-eyed wonder and amusement, as if we were little boys from Mars.

"Helen," he said warily to my mother, "they might be better off if they rolled them pants up. I'd hate to see 'em get all wet."

So we took off our shoes and socks and rolled up our lime green or tangerine orlon pants to just below the knee.

"You're in charge of the bailer," Phil said as he handed me an old tin can. "You gotta make sure we don't sink out there."

I eyed the leaky boat. It already had three inches of water in the bottom.

"Don't scare 'em, Phil," said Lil. "They never been out on a boat before!"

Too late. I was already calculating the odds on my death. Would I rather expose myself as a coward in front of my brother, who was four years older and much braver, or commit myself to almost certain death by drowning? I stepped resolutely into the little Titanic and started to bail energetically.

"Not yet," said Phil. "Wait'll we get out a ways."

The wire pots, baited with fish heads, each had six or so crabs in them, along with the other detritus that had floated through. We shook them out into the bottom of the boat and kept only the big ones — No. 1 Jimmies — and freed the females and smaller males to scavenge another day. Under Phil's gentle instruction, we were transformed from little princes into boys, nicking our fingers, staining and tearing our clothes, cursing mildly, and spitting often into the vast gray-brown expanse of the bay.

As a break from the lifting, emptying, and rebaiting of the crab pots, Phil suggested we try a little fishing, although he explained to us that this wasn't the best time of day for it. He carried a rod with him in the boat and a box with tackle and some worms. If we caught anything, he said, we could cut off the heads and use them to bait the crab pots. He showed us how to bait the hook so that the worm wouldn't get nibbled off too easily, and he cast the line in a wide arc into the bay.

"I doubt they're hungry, but you never know," he said. "We'll see if we can't get 'em to nibble a little." He made it seem as if he were feeding these friends of his, not catching them for dinner. He wasn't a hunter but a partner in a slow dance of seduction. He cast the line out a few more times and slowly reeled it in. We sat very quietly so as not to warn the fish.

"No, they don't want to eat right now. Them fish are lazy."

And so was he; and so were we. The boat drifted aimlessly, without anchor. Phil's eyes looked far into the distance, past the fishing line, past the horizon, past time. His face had a look of sleepy satisfaction; his mouth smiled knowingly as if it knew a secret. He nodded softly to himself, agreeing with the thoughts that swam and scuttled through his mind. Ed and I drifted off into our own reveries; the little-boy tensions that we carried onto the boat slowly sank into the deep, fishy waters of the bay, down to the sandy bottom. As the August sun slid close to the horizon and the water turned all orange and steamy, we headed for home, dirty and happy, with no fish but with hundreds of angry blue crabs snapping angrily inches away from our toes.

That night at the cabin, Phil and his son-in-law Fred emptied a couple bottles each of beer and malt vinegar into an impossibly large kettle, fashioned a wire rack above the liquid, and then laid the crabs in layer on heavily spiced layer. First crabs, then kosher salt, then cayenne, then a local product called Old Bay Seasoning, then more crabs. Fred took an ice pick and stuck the crabs through the top shell — not to kill them; crabs must be steamed live — but to stun them a little so that they didn't tear each other's claws off. When the pot was full, they put the top on, and a cinder block on top of that to block off any hope of escape, and lit the fire. We kids listened with unconflicted glee to the last desperate movements of the crabs as the pot filled with steam, not a Buddhist among us.

The women covered the long table with newspaper many layers thick and set out paring knives and wooden mallets at each place, and several bowls of cold pickled onions to cut the bite of the pepper. A keg of beer was tapped, and the first kettleful of red, peppery, steaming-hot crabs was turned onto the center of the table. There was much shouting and joking as we each tried to single out the biggest, heaviest crab. "No shopping. If you touch it, you bought it." I can't recall ever seeing happier, more expectant faces than those around that table. I sat quietly so that no one would notice that it was already well past my usual bedtime. The cooking hadn't gotten under way until after nine, and by now it was edging toward eleven. But nobody seemed to take notice.

We started in, slowly and meticulously, arguing over the best way to extract the most meat with the least effort. Everybody had a foolproof method; everybody was an expert. Lil tore the claws off and kept them off to the side to eat later.

"I like to save the best for last," she said. "When nobody has any claws left, you'll all be beggin' me for 'em." She was right. If you hit the claw in exactly the right place with the mallet, the entire shell pulled away in one piece and left a perfectly formed finger of claw meat just the right size for a mouthful. I watched Lil's pile of claws grow as the evening progressed. She watched me watching and winked at me every now and then as if to say, "Don't worry, honey, your Aunt Lil'll take care of you."

My parents seemed to metamorphose into simpler people as they dug into the crabs. The tension between them eased. Maybe all that pounding on the crab shells lessened their need to hit on each other. Maybe getting away from their respective families relieved them of the obligation to put each other down all the time. I could feel a palpable physical attraction between them as they sat around the table. Their Baltimore accents broadened a little; my dad told a joke about these nuns in a convent who were harvesting cucumbers in their garden, and as a nun was bragging about the size of one, holding her hands out to show the measurement, another nun who was hard of hearing asked, "Father who?" My mom's laughter bubbled over the top even as she shook her head with disapproval. She seemed to forget that Ed and I were there at all, which was just fine with us.

"Gawd, Henery," chimed in Lil. "Can't take you anywhere!"

"She thought they were talkin' about the priest!" yelled Phil and he choked on his laughter, his face turning as red as the crabs. The room rocked with laughter again and again, and another kettle of crabs was poured onto the newspaper and produced, miraculously, an even larger pile of empty shells.

We ate on and on into the night, the pepper caked around our mouths, on our hands and arms right up to the elbows. Phil encouraged Ed and me to sip a little beer to cool the fire on our tongues. My mom, who was leaning against my dad's arm in tipsy affection, nodded her approval. I couldn't believe it. My head buzzed, my mouth was on fire, my fingers smarted with the little nicks and cuts from opening the crabs. I was in heaven. And then, as yet another huge kettle was dumped onto the newspaper, we all agreed that these were, indeed, the best we had ever tasted, the freshest, the meatiest, the most succulent ever.

When we started to slow down — at about 2:30 or 3:00 in the morning — the smell of fresh coffee, bacon, and eggs drifted over from the stove. Lil was dishing up breakfast for the fishermen, me included, who needed a hot breakfast before sailing out to catch the dawn.

Never before had I broken so many rules — skipping bed, sipping beer, eating two meals in a row. Never before had I lived outside of time, outside of structure. Never before had I been so happy. I think this is my earliest memory of pleasurable eating, and it set a high standard for the rest of my life.

I've repeated this feast many times over the years, ordering bushels of live blue crabs mail order. The one I remember best was about ten years ago in New York when I was challenged by David Liederman, the Cookie King, to make him a dinner that he had never eaten before. After four solid hours of malleting, picking, and gorging, he pronounced it the "greatest prolonged chew" of his life. Instead of ending with breakfast, I topped off the meal with real Maryland crab cakes. I say real because they don't contain any little bits of green or red pepper, or worse yet, get rolled in bread crumbs and sautéed in butter. No. The secret — or shall I say sleight of hand — with these perfect crab cakes is that they seem to contain nothing but large, firm chunks of crab, held together by nothing but desire. This is not true, of course, but they do give that impression.

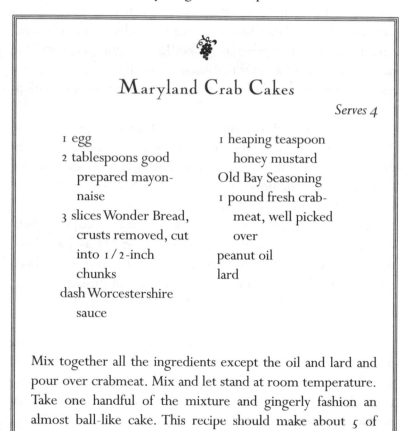

Maryland Crab Cakes

Serves 4

1 egg
2 tablespoons good
   prepared mayon-
   naise
3 slices Wonder Bread,
   crusts removed, cut
   into 1/2-inch
   chunks
dash Worcestershire
   sauce

1 heaping teaspoon
   honey mustard
Old Bay Seasoning
1 pound fresh crab-
   meat, well picked
   over
peanut oil
lard

Mix together all the ingredients except the oil and lard and pour over crabmeat. Mix and let stand at room temperature. Take one handful of the mixture and gingerly fashion an almost ball-like cake. This recipe should make about 5 of them. Fry in a large cast-iron skillet in the oil and lard, which should be about an inch deep in the skillet. Don't try to get fancy with these ingredients. Wonder Bread works because it has virtually no character — it disappears without a trace!

Serve with additional honey mustard or Worcestershire sauce or just the way they are.

ॐ

Klein's

 During the summer vacations when I was in high school I worked for my Uncle Benny at the National Wholesale Jewelry Company. My main job was delivering watches and jewelry to the various repair shops in the neighborhood. This was old, mercantile Baltimore, the area that was plowed under to make way for Harbor Place and all the urban revitalization that has supplanted the town I grew up in.

My job was one of grave responsibility. I carried expensive, sometimes priceless, pieces of jewelry through the rough streets, up dark stairways, through back alleys, wherever the jewelry artisans' cubbyholes were hidden away.

Uncle Benny checked my pockets for holes every morning, then put both his hands on my shoulders and very gravely instructed me to be on guard at all times. I had seen the wholesale jewelry salesmen from New York come and go dressed in the long black coats and full beards of Hassidic Jews, with their black leather cases ominously handcuffed to their wrists. I had heard the stories of hairy Jewish hands being cut off for the treasure trove of diamonds and emeralds that they carried. So I understood the need for security. I always put the goods in my right pocket with my hand jammed in firmly on top. I walked briskly, but not so fast as to attract attention. I never used the same route twice, and I often stopped, pretended to tie my shoe, and then doubled back to confound any potential international jewel thief that might be following me. It was a great job.

My other responsibilities included sweeping up, supervising the unloading of deliveries of larger items like clocks and small appliances, and getting lunch for the salesmen, who, because they worked on commission, never left the floor from 8:00 A.M. to closing. At lunchtime I would take food orders and then head down to the end of the block and up a flight of stairs to Klein's Billiard Academy.

It was a large room with a plain wooden floor and two huge commercial windows at the front end — to your right as you went up the stairs. The ceiling was old tin painted dark brown, with large, lazily rotating ceiling fans. There were twenty or so old-style pool tables with leather pockets and carved mahogany frames that were nearly silent in action. And at the far end was a long L-shaped counter behind which was a nondescript steam table that served up the finest sandwiches I have ever eaten. No famous New York deli or Montreal smoked-meat counter or Rotterdam broodjes shop has ever put together a tastier, moister, more generously sliced sandwich than did the counter-men at Klein's. I have searched. I have tasted them all, but I doubt there ever was or ever will be a better brisket sandwich than I had at that august establishment.

I was lucky they let me in. If I hadn't been carrying back sandwiches for the men at Benny's store, I would have been unceremoniously kicked back down the stairs, for there were no kids at Klein's. No women. No pool hustlers. No ne'er-do-wells. Only men of business, bankers, and brokers — the burghers of Baltimore, their suit coats folded carefully over the backs of the tall stools that lined the walls.

I got my sandwich first, then put in my order for the rest and waited in the darkest, least conspicuous corner and watched. I tried to eat as slowly as possible, to make it last — the thick slices of incredibly succulent, barely-holding-together beefy brisket between hand-cut slices of seeded rye bread slathered with pungent horseradish mustard. It was no use. I couldn't slow myself down. The sandwich was gone before I wanted it to be, before I even started to sip the cream soda that I had bought to pace myself. Pleasure like that wasn't made to last — not for me. Not then; not now. Like the excruciating moment in the throes of passion when she begs you, "Don't stop. . . . Don't! . . ." Ah, well. And I hadn't even thought of stopping until she brought it up.

The men, in their variously colored shirts, some with suspenders like bright badges blazoning their individuality, cigars or cigarettes dangling from their lips, lines of concentration creasing their foreheads, played a serious game. They spoke to one another without looking, focusing all their attention on the green table between them. They said things to the table they would never dream of saying to each other's face. It was a performance, a dance with cue and chalk, a strut.

I watched them with wonder, these paunchy, middle-aged men playing at gambler, gangster, gigolo, and tough — until lunchtime was over and the Negro porter brushed their suit jackets off with his whisk broom, helped them on with them, and sent them back down the stairs to become accountant, salesman, haberdasher, and clerk. Klein's was a magic place.

*   *   *

The allure of brisket of beef, or corned beef, simmered in boiling aromatic water or broth is not singular to Jewish delis or sandwich counters. Whenever I read about the eating habits of great chefs, there's always a mention of boiled beef with perhaps a little horseradish on the side as the favorite dish to savor after a busy day of preparing far fancier dishes for their clientele. In fact, most people in the know consider this method the best for producing the perfect taste in a really good piece of meat — far better than broiling, roasting, or sautéing. One of the first meals I ate in Rome was at the legendary D'al Bolognese in the Piazza d'el Poppolo, which is one of the few places in Rome where the classic bollito misto is still served. It contained a chicken and other cuts of meat such as tongue, but its centerpiece was a steaming chunk of perfectly boiled brisket that spun me back decades to the incomparable sandwich at Klein's.

There is an oft-told story in gourmet circles — I must have seen it in a dozen cookbooks in one version or another — about the Prince of Eurasia and the famous French gastronome Dodin-Bouffant. It seems the prince wanted to impress the Frenchman and presented him with a meal of embarrassing vulgarity and excess. Dodin-Bouffant returned the invitation, and when the prince and his friends showed up — all atwitter in anticipation of a major blowout dinner — the menu was announced: "Boiled beef with vegetables." That was it. Ready to be bitterly disappointed, insulted, perhaps enraged enough to declare war, the prince waited for this meager meal. But when it was served, the prince and all his sycophants realized why Dodin-Bouffant was the acknowledged master of all cooking-dom. As the slices of meat were cut, the mouth-watering texture could actually be seen; as the aroma permeated their nostrils, they knew what a feast they were in for . . . and so on and so forth. I think the prince made Dodin-Bouffant a duke, or gave him half his fortune. It doesn't really matter; the important thing is the transcendent quality of the boiled beef — transcendent because that Eurasian prince and that part-time delivery boy (me) had the same experience centuries apart when a knife eased its way through a particularly juicy chunk of brisket.

From Italians and their bollito misto to the French and their pot-au-feu; from the Germans and their rindfleisch to the Irish with corned beef and cabbage, everyone agrees on a few basics of the perfect boiled beef. One: It is not boiled; it is simmered at the merest possible simmer. If the water boils, turn it down; if it becomes altogether still, turn it up a little. Find the gentlest definition of simmer that your stove can manage. Two: Skim off the scum. That's the word everybody uses, and it seems to be the one cooking by-product that no one has found a secondary use for. I've yet to see, "Set scum aside for that little risotto tomorrow." Three: The water must already be boiling (simmering) when you add the meat. If you put the meat in cold water and then start to heat it, you impart the best taste into what becomes the broth. The proper way is to lock the flavors in by adding it directly to the already bubbling, aromatic water. Some recipes for corned beef eschew this wisdom, but I am sure it's right. Four (and this may be the most important): The succulent texture that I remember from Klein's — and that the prince remembered from Dodin-Bouffant's — does not live long after the beef is lifted from its simmering liquid. This is agreed upon by every expert I've come across and further proved by every bad piece of brisket I've eaten at my Aunt Ida's that's been sitting on a plate for a half hour. It loses its magic.

The slicer at Klein's prepared the bread with mustard first. Then, with his long-handled fork, he raised the steaming brisket out of the kettle, sliced it immediately, and handed you your sandwich. You didn't wait; you ate it there and then — ambrosia. The salesmen back at Uncle Benny's store who had to wait while I watched the pool players never got what they were paying for. The magic moment was long gone. They had only a meat sandwich and not the transcendent culinary miracle that the prince and I just had up at Klein's a few minutes before. I'd like to take this opportunity to apologize to them.

THREE

Jerry's P.K.s

🍇

It loomed as the single most important event of my
life. Granted, at seventeen almost everything seemed important; will I have to go to summer school to make up math,
science, history, and mechanical drawing? Should Red China
be admitted to the United Nations? Will I get under Gail Gar-
ner's brassiere? But this was more. This was potentially life
changing. On Saturday at 11:30 A.M. in New York City, I would
give my audition before the vaunted faculty of Carnegie Tech's
drama department, and if successful, I would be on my way
to join the ranks of the unemployed professional acting community. If not, given my dismal grade point average and lack-
luster college boards, I would hop a freighter and sail around the
world to become the first-ever middle-class Jewish soldier of
fortune. There was a lot at stake. Fortunately, I had an ally.

If you're lucky, you get one great teacher in your life who
changes your perspective on everything. If you're lucky, he or
she comes along at a time when the world seems overwhelm-
ingly confusing and intimidating, and with the wave of a hand,

or the opening of a book, simplifies things, clarifies them, and makes you feel eager to challenge the world and conquer it. Good teachers are magicians, sleight-of-hand artists; they find energy and excitement where none existed before. Such a teacher was Jerry Levin for me. I met him in tenth-grade English class. He looked barely old enough to be out of college, and his demeanor was even more boyish than his looks. The first thing he did was make it clear that he was cooler and badder than anybody in the class, and we learned quickly that this was no pose. Some smart-ass mouthed off right at the top of the hour and Jerry just threw him out of class.

"Where do I go?" asked the boy.

"I don't care," said Jerry, "I just don't want you in here." And he shut the door behind him. The boy opened the door again.

"Should I go to the office?"

"No, they don't want you there either," said Jerry.

We saw the boy pacing back and forth in front of the door with increasing confusion and anxiety for the rest of the hour. He never mouthed off again.

But Jerry did. About Shakespeare and Dylan Thomas and *The Catcher in the Rye*. He set my head spinning at such a pace, it hasn't stopped yet. Sentence structure, punctuation, metaphors and similes (metties and simmies to Jerry), he made me want to learn everything there was to learn about reading, writing, and speaking the English language. He dazzled me with the nuances of words, the intricate set of rules governing the use of those words, and the consummate joy of breaking those rules for the perfect dramatic effect. I wanted to learn it all. And this from a boy who hadn't wanted to learn anything before and learned little else after. But I wanted to learn to please him, and I did.

I read Sir Andrew Aguecheek to his Sir Toby Belch from

Twelfth Night, to the squealing delight of the class, and first realized that acting Shakespeare is the same as acting anything else,
except that the writing is better. I read Dylan Thomas's *Fern Hill*
to the class and learned that I could quiet a large audience
simply by touching my own emotions. It was in Jerry's class that
I first tasted the power an actor can hold if he has great words
to say.

Jerry also played the banjo and ran the folksinging club,
which met after school. I joined and learned how to become a
bohemian. I drank coffee and grew my hair longer and found
great soulful significance in singing about having a little dog
whose name was Blue. I stretched my boundaries.

The year passed and I went on to other English classes, but
Jerry and I remained in touch. We became friends. He followed
with proprietary interest as I acted in the school plays and community theater productions around town. He was the only one
who took my aspirations seriously, so when in my senior year I
was in his class again, he and I plotted my future behind the
backs of my parents and the school's guidance counselor. They
all saw me squeaking into the University of Maryland, which
pretty much had to take me if I managed to graduate from high
school. They saw me staying close to home, repeating the lives
and careers of the friends of my parents and their offspring, aspiring only to what I could see and what I could touch and what
had gone before. But Jerry and I had a different plan. I would be
an actor. It was clearly the only career I had any talent for and it
was the only chance I had to escape the intense gravitational
force of northwest Baltimore.

We found the best drama department in the country, which
at that time was Carnegie Tech in Pittsburgh. We learned that if
I could show them an impressive enough audition, my shameful

academic history would not hold me back. We chose audition pieces — one serious and one comic. They were to be no longer than three minutes apiece and demonstrate that I had some versatility. The serious piece was from *Blue Denim,* a mawkish drama of teenage pregnancy, which in 1962 seemed to be as serious as teenage problems could get. I played the role of the best friend of our hero — a role I would go on to play many times in my career — and acted a monologue in which I learn of my friend's self-control problems. I remember my jaw dropping a lot. The second piece was a lot more fun. *Fumed Oak* is a Noel Coward one-acter in which a downtrodden, henpecked husband, father, and son-in-law explodes in a delightful worm-turning speech, tells his wife, daughter, and mother-in-law what he thinks of them all, and walks out the door to begin a new life. It's a scenery-chewing gem, and I could trot out my Rex Harrison imitation, which I copied meticulously from the original cast album of *My Fair Lady.*

We honed the monologues down to three perfect minutes apiece; we completed the application forms and received word that the auditions were to take place in New York. My parents, the guidance counselor, my friends, all humored me, not imagining that I could get into Carnegie Tech, which they thought was just an engineering school and far beyond my reach academically. But I knew I could do it. Because I had to. This school was the one tiny chink in the impenetrable wall of show business. It was my only way in.

So imagine if you can my excitement as the big weekend approached. Not only was my whole future at stake, but I was going to New York with Jerry Levin, who was without a doubt the coolest human being who ever lived. He was smart and hip, an outlaw among academics, and most impressive, a romancer of exotic women. I was always amazed that these women found their way to Baltimore. Where did he find them? He was dating Doris in those days. She was very tall and had short-cropped red hair and spoke in a thick German accent. It was the first time I had ever considered that a German accent could be anything other than sinister. Hers was actually cute. And sexy. I can't recall what Doris did for a living. I want to say that she was a lingerie model, but I think that's just wish fulfillment. Probably not a brain surgeon — she had too much free time in the afternoons. I had serious fantasies about Doris then and for years after — visions of black leather garter belts with swastikas, of red-painted pointed fingernails torturing me with a long feather. Doris was great.

So Mike and Jerry, poets of love, performers extraordinaire, bon vivants, took on the big city. We arrived Friday evening on the train, tap-danced down the ramp at Penn Station singing "Meetcha at the station at a quarter to nine . . . ," had a fancy dinner at a Mafia hangout in lower Manhattan, and saw a Broadway show. So far, so good. Jerry had the plans for the next night well in hand; we would have dinner in the Bronx at the apartment of an old army buddy and then go to the Village to hear Ian and Sylvia at the Bitter End. It was all vague in my mind, as I was concentrating on the audition.

We went back to the hotel and I laid out my three-piece suit like a matador the night before he fights the bravest bull. I cleansed my body, I purified my soul, I purged my spirit. I went over my lines. I lay there, unable to sleep. I listened to the city pulsating, never sleeping . . . my kind of town.

The audition was a triumph, in my mind at least. I saw myself transforming from pimply teenager to portly Britisher right before their awestruck eyes. I was in a state of grace. Like that moment when your car spins out of control on the ice and time seems to slow down and everything clarifies as it passes before your eyes. That was the feeling I had during the audition. Of course this would be my career! It was a calling; I was touched by the muse. As I finished the audition, I glanced at my audience. I noticed that they had managed to cover the look of slack-jawed reverence on their faces with feigned nonchalance. But I knew.

I spent the rest of the afternoon in a bubble, floating around the Broadway area, taking in the sights of my future stomping grounds. Jerry kept a running patter: "And here we have Sardi's, where Mr. Tucker sips his dry martini after his triumphant portrayal of Hamlet at the Martin Beck Theater. . . ." We bought a *Variety* and read it over coffee at the Stage Deli. I have never been so high, or so full of myself.

During the subway ride out to the Bronx that night, Jerry caught me up on where we were headed. Freddy Blassevick and Jerry had been in the army together and become great pals. Whenever Jerry went to New York, he headed for Freddy's mother's apartment in the Bronx for "Mrs. B.'s P.K.s," which turned out to be potato pancakes made from an old Blassevick family recipe. I don't know exactly how Jerry got the initials *P.K.* from potato pancake, but P.K.s they were, and I wasn't about to question my English teacher on matters of spelling. I felt miffed at having to leave my beloved Manhattan for the wilds of some unknown, untheatrical borough. But Jerry had been so generous to me that I couldn't begrudge him a little time to see some old friends before we returned to Manhattan, or My Town, as I thought of it by then.

We walked about three blocks from the subway in the arctic February night. I remember a lot of overturned trash cans outside block-long apartment buildings that all seemed the same — monoliths with dingy yellow bricks and small, dimly lit windows. The streets echoed with unknown and faintly threatening sounds — sirens, garbage trucks, the constant rumble of the subway beneath us. "Come on, Jerry!" I begged in silence, "let's blow this borough. Manhattan waits for no man!" I felt my perfect day losing some of its momentum.

Mrs. Blassevick's apartment was small and the radiators were pumping out heat full blast. We collected in the kitchen, where she was in the middle of grating potatoes and onions for the famous P.K.s. Freddy and his sister were at the table having a beer; Jerry joined them and offered me one. I nodded. What the hell. After a few sips, I felt heat rising up out of the black turtleneck sweater that I had bought for our trip to the Village later that night. The warmth of the kitchen and the beer began to work on my brain. "Hey!" I wanted to scream, "what about my martini at Sardi's and the Martin Beck Theater?" My day of days was slipping away and Jerry along with it. He was focusing all his attention and his charm on these other people — these Bronx people — and none at all on me. "What about my audition, for Christ's sake?" I couldn't believe we had stopped talking about my audition already. I wasn't anywhere near ready to let it go.

And as their banter grew, I receded further and further into the background to brood, like Hamlet. If I couldn't be the center of attention, I thought, I would be the artist — alone, alienated — the observer taking notes for future reference, for future roles. "There's Jerry," I thought, existentially, "the master of ceremonies, the jester; watch him work the room." I noted how he kept a constant patter going with Freddy — old jokes, memories, songs they once sang together. I watched him flatter the whole Blassevick family with his attention. And they loved it. Especially Freddy's sister — I can't remember her name, only that she was a friend of a friend of Theodore Bikel and that she was very beautiful. I watched her eyes shine as Jerry teased her — like a big brother, I noted, and *not* like a big brother. I watched her fall in love, and hide her love.

I couldn't help but observe Mrs. Blassevick, now in the midst of frying up the P.K.s. She was radiant under the spell of Jerry's praise and direction. Her apron, dotted with grease, patterned with pansies, was edged with frilly white lace and seemed no bigger than a pocket handkerchief on her generous frame. Her face was flushed with excitement and Jerry's flattery — and from the fact that she was standing over a huge cast-iron skillet bubbling with rendered chicken fat.

As the P.K.s were lifted onto the brown shopping-bag paper to drain off some of the fat, the room was mobilized — plates and silverware, applesauce, sour cream, more beer; Jerry and the Blassevicks flew into their act, laughing, singing the "Latke Song," an ancient, traditional paean to potato pancakes.

But I was outside the fun. I don't know if it was the beer or my jealousy or my new-found feeling of artistic objectivity, but I was definitely not a participant. Jerry sensed it and without missing a beat managed to fold me into the proceedings. He made an occasion out of it, as was his style — always.

"We have a latke virgin in our midst! An initiate into the mysterious rite of Mrs. B.'s P.K.s! A little drumroll, please." And they all pounded on the metal kitchen table, rattling the dishes.

"Applesauce or sour cream," said Jerry, "the age-old question." And he placed a bowl of each on either side of a plate of sizzling P.K.s.

And as I dipped my pancake first into one, then into the other, voluptuously taste testing the crunchy potato-onion-chicken-fat experience juxtaposed first against the baby-food sweet texture of the applesauce, then against the more sophisticated creamy coldness of the sour cream, all self-consciousness and jealousy and artistic objectivity fell away. It's hard to be Hamlet with a potato pancake in your hand. As I reached for another and another, the warmth rose and the chicken fat melted my heart.

"You haven't told these guys about your audition yet," said Jerry. "This guy made show business history today."

Tell them? I could do better than that. I had Jerry help me move the table and chairs back to the wall and we created a tiny theater in the Blassevick kitchen. They all got themselves another bottle of beer and Mrs. B. turned the flame way down under the P.K.s. I waited until all the bustle stopped, until they were seated and quiet. Then I waited another moment — for dramatic effect.

I've performed on many stages over the years since that weekend. First at Carnegie Tech (the audition was successful), then in theaters big and small all over the country, but never has there been a more receptive audience than I had that night in the Bronx. They sat in rapt silence during the serious piece, and roared with laughter at the comedy. There was even an intermission so that Mrs. B. could drain the next batch of P.K.s. And afterward there was a thunderous ovation, with cheers and whistles and beer bottles banging on the metal table. I could have taken three more bows, at least. When the cheers subsided, Mrs. Blassevick came up to me, her eyes shining with pride — as if I were her own son.

"Just like a real actor," she said. Which may be the best review I've ever received.

Mrs. B.'s P.K.s

Serves 6

To be completely honest, this isn't Mrs. B.'s actual recipe. This is the result of painstaking trial and error of almost every recipe for potato pancakes I could find — excepting of course Irish potato pancakes, which are a whole separate animal and don't even include onions. Add to that my considerable food memory of P.K.s past: Mrs. B.'s, my mom's, Carnegie Deli's, and others. Special thanks to David "the Latke King" Firestone, whose wonderful recipe appeared in Molly O'Neill's *New York Cookbook*. I've gone with matzo meal rather than flour for a more substantial texture, and with great regret I've left out the chicken fat as an additive for the frying medium — not only for health reasons but also because it makes your kitchen smell like the Bronx for three days.

6 large unpeeled Idaho potatoes	a handful chopped parsley
1 large yellow onion	salt and freshly ground pepper
2 eggs, lightly beaten	2 cups olive oil
1/4 cup matzo meal	

Shred the potatoes either by hand with the coarse side of a grater or with the shredding disk of a food processor.

Grate the onions on the same coarse grater. Combine with

the potatoes, then drain the potato-onion mixture in a colander. Squeeze out the excess moisture.

Return the potato-onion mixture to a bowl and add the eggs, matzo meal, parsley, salt, and pepper. Stir.

Heat the oil in a large skillet until quite hot. Slide in large spoonfuls of the pancake mixture. Flatten them and reduce the heat.

Cook the pancakes until golden brown, then turn them and cook the other side. Drain on brown paper bags.

ॐ

Pittsburgh

I learned a lot my freshman year of college. First of all, I discovered that I functioned more successfully on my own than I ever did at home; I was born to be my own boss. I learned how as an actor I had to travel a different road from other people; that I had to open myself up to all the possibilities; that I was capable of being all people, of feeling every emotion. I loved the idea of being different, special, of using my body, mind, and imagination as an instrument — like a musician uses a violin — to express myself. It was very romantic, this artist business. And I learned that I would rather die than eat on the freshman food plan.

The very name was an affront to my sensibilities. Food is not a plan, it's a celebration, an indulgence, a sensually gratifying event. If they had called it the freshman sensual indulgence maybe I would have given it a shot, but I don't think so. It was at this time that I developed a theory that has stayed with me to this day: there are only a finite number of meals left in life — don't waste one. If the food isn't palatable, if it isn't exciting or engaging in some way, skip it and wait for a better meal.

So I called my dad and made a proposal. I asked him to take the money he was putting into the wretched food plan and give it to me. I told him to give me *less* than the food plan — my dad always liked a deal. I assured him I would feed myself better and learn how to manage my money in the bargain. He went for it. He deposited the food money every month into a checking account that had already been set up for my meager weekly allowance, and I was on my own.

Then came an event that not only reshaped the world but also had a powerful effect on me personally — the Cuban missile crisis. It was to become a watershed event in my life — politically, economically, and gastronomically. I first heard about it as I left Scobell Hall (my dorm) on the way to crew. Crew was not an intramural rowing society but a form of enforced slave labor created by the drama department in order to get its scenery built. Crew was required for all freshmen, and I hated it almost as much as the freshman food plan. We had to construct flats out of lumber and muslin, and paint them with sizing to stretch them tight. We had to hang twenty-ton pieces of scenery from the fly gallery and hoist them up and down. We had to learn to use ratchets and power saws and other instruments of torture. We had to get dust in our sinuses. I was never built for manual labor; that's why I became an actor in the first place. But crew was required for credit, and there was no ducking it.

As I walked down the grass hill in front of my dorm, I saw Tom Dement waving to me to wait up. He was walking up fast from Forbes Avenue, where he lived in a rooming house off campus. Tom was older than all the other freshmen — about twenty-five, I think. And he was fatter, too. He went about 280 pounds, and the sight of him moving so quickly was a rare one.

Tom had already been out in the world. He had worked professionally as an actor at the Karamu Playhouse in Cleveland and had come back to school to pick up a degree in directing. Sometimes he laid it on a bit thick about how much more he knew about everything, but the fact is, he *did* know more. He had latched onto me and a few other actors, directors, and writers that he considered promising and established himself as the éminence grise among us. He often presided at all-night discussions at a coffee shop down in the Oakland section near the University of Pittsburgh. The rest of us would soak up his scholarly dissertations on existentialism, Peter Brook, and Bertolt Brecht while our brains short-circuited on coffee. One of us would always pick up Tom's tab, but it was worth it. Since he had been a professional actor, we all accepted the fact that he was terminally broke.

Anyway, here he was, huffing and puffing up the street, calling for me to wait.

"You heard about Kennedy?"

"What?"

"He's setting up an embargo around Cuba. He's gonna forcibly stop any Soviet ship that's carrying missiles."

"Good for him," I said ignorantly. I had no idea what was going on, but I loved Kennedy; anything he wanted to do was okay with me.

"Tell me how good it is when Pittsburgh gets fried — along with every other major city in the country. Khrushchev's not backing down, you know."

I felt that little amoeba of panic that had lived inside

my stomach ever since I went through those air-raid drills in elementary school. Along with every other kid who grew up in the fifties, I knew deep down inside that we would all get blown to hell by an ICBM someday.

"They're not gonna drop any bombs," I said, the panic rising. Tom just raised his eyes to heaven. Then he bummed a cigarette from me, which he placed in an elegant cigarette holder that he always used. For a guy who never changed his socks, he had some pretty fancy habits.

"Let's find a TV," he suggested.

"I'm late for crew," I said. "One more time and they flunk me." I was on the verge of being the first person ever to lose an undergraduate degree for failing to hammer.

We walked over to the theater, passing groups of students standing around transistor radios, glumly following the news. When we got to the drama department, the door was locked and a sign said all activities were canceled.

"Jesus. They shut down crew."

This was a first. I had conflicting emotions. I was exhilarated by the fact that I wouldn't have to work and numbed by the knowledge that I would be incinerated within a few hours. We walked over to Skibo, the student union, and watched Walter Cronkite for a while. He didn't like the situation any more than Tom did.

"Lets get a real meal," said Tom suddenly. The emotion he put into the word *real,* plus the grim, determined, existential-hero look on his face, left no doubt that he was talking about our last meal — perhaps the last meal for all life on this planet. He held my eye to let it sink in.

"Where?"

"Steak at Joseph's!"

His face suddenly changed to that of a mischievous boy, up to no good and very pleased with himself. Now, I had never been to Joseph's and probably neither had Tom. It was known for the best and biggest steaks, and prices to match.

"How will we pay for it?" I asked. I had a couple of bucks in my pocket and was sure that Tom had less. If he had had any money, he wouldn't have been there. He would have been off eating somewhere.

"They take checks," said Tom. He knew the world. We walked back to the dorm, where I picked up my checkbook.

"Should I get dressed?"

Tom shrugged as if to say, "What does it matter?"

At Joseph's there was an eerie, end-of-the-world kind of feeling; nobody looked twice at us as we walked in. The TV was on in the bar and everyone was glued to one of those round-the-clock crisis news broadcasts. The hostess didn't even ask if we had reservations and sat us right down. She asked what we wanted to drink. Tom spread his arms out wide, took a deep breath, then rubbed his palms together briskly, closed his eyes, and let the breath out in a long slow stream. He seemed about to go into a mystic trance. The waitress and I waited quietly. Finally, he opened his eyes, smiled, and said, "Whiskey sour." She looked over to me. I just nodded as if to say, "That's okay with me." I was only eighteen, although very mature looking. I thought if I didn't speak, I might get away with it. "Two whiskey sours," she said without missing a beat, and went off to the bar. I guess she figured if I was old enough to die, I was old enough to drink. It was that kind of night.

Along with the drinks, the waitress brought a basket of garlic bread with cheese melted on top. We munched on it, slowly perused the menu, and ordered another round. Tom was completely absorbed in the menu. He read it over and over, making sure not to miss anything.

"You ready, or you want to look some more?" asked the waitress.

"Not quite," said Tom, and ordered yet another round of whiskey sours.

He inserted another of my cigarettes into his holder, lit up, and took a long pull on his drink. He looked very happy. I was feeling pretty good myself. By the time the waitress brought the third round of drinks, I was a hell of a lot more sanguine about the end of the world. "If it's time, then it's time," I thought. "What the hell."

"I'm ready now," announced Tom.

The waitress waited, pencil poised, as Tom looked over the whole menu one more time. This being our last meal, there was a lot of pressure to get it just right.

"Now, this double porterhouse for two . . . ?"

"That's our best steak," said the waitress.

"Can it be ordered for one?"

To her credit, she barely paused. "Sure, hon. You're the boss."

"Medium rare," said Tom, and he raised his whiskey sour glass, pinkie aloft, and smugly tilted his head back and forth as if to say, "What a good boy am I."

They both looked over at me.

"Sounds great. Medium rare." We had now ordered half a cow. She turned back to Tom, who was obviously in charge.

"We have twice-baked potato or french fries."

Tom made a circular gesture with his hand that very clearly indicated "all of the above." The waitress looked at me and I nodded. "And a double order of broccoli with cheese sauce," said Tom, making that circular gesture again. "For the table. That'll be your greens," he said, peering over his glasses, suddenly parental. I didn't understand why we had to worry about a balanced meal if we weren't expecting to live through the night, but I didn't argue.

"Will that do it?"

"I think we need some onion rings," I said, getting into the swing of it. "A double order. For the table," and I practiced my circular gesture.

"Grilled tomatoes?" asked Tom.

"Absolutely," said I.

The meal progressed at a stately, almost reverential pace. Tom savored every mouthful of steak, cutting the pieces ever smaller to make it last longer. We artfully designed each bite: a piece of steak with just a tad of fat for extra flavor, an onion ring, twirled tightly, and a sweet morsel of grilled tomato; then onions and tomato only — the vegetarian bite —then broccoli with cheese sauce and onion. The permutations seemed endless. And another round of drinks.

We finished with a pot of fresh-brewed coffee and cheesecake — only one slice apiece.

When the bill came, I wrote out the check. It wiped me out for a month. "God," I thought through the haze, "If Khrushchev backs down and there's no nuclear holocaust, I'm fucked." And of course that proved to be the case. But I learned another lesson. This was a year for lessons, as I have said. I learned I could face death. I could stare stone-faced into the eyes of the Grim Reaper and stand my ground. And I learned, when faced with the choice of twice-baked potato or fries, go for both.

It was a year later, in my sophomore year, that I really started to cook. I had done a little cooking at home out of self-preservation. In order to dodge my mother's culinary hockey pucks, I experimented in replicating junk food — an endeavor that I've well nigh perfected in my late forties. I knocked off Big Macs, cheese-steak hoagies, and pizza. And I took the grilled cheese sandwich to a level theretofore unheard of.

But my cooking didn't really become sophisticated until I got a call from my mother with one of those requests I usually run from. She told me I had to get in touch with a cousin of mine who was also in Pittsburgh at the time. Warning bells went off in my brain; cousins mean dark mildewy apartments with platters of pimply, boiled chicken, limp carrots, and gray peas. "It's Philip Glass," said my mother. "Your cousin Joy's husband's brother. Call him."

And I did. And Philip turned out to be not your typical cousin at all. He was just what I needed at that moment in my life. Philip, who was shortly to become a renowned composer of modern music, was off and running into the next phase of life — the one that was just peeking over the horizon for me. He had just graduated from Juilliard and was composing music on a Ford Foundation grant for the Pittsburgh public schools. He was in that phase between school and life — a sort of limbo that exists when money hasn't yet become a serious necessity and the future is too far away to worry about. And he was a very romantic figure. He opened up new possibilities for this middle-class boy from suburban Baltimore. He showed me how to live like an artist. He lived alone — in a working-men's neighborhood in East Liberty — in a fourth-floor walk-up. He read French authors. He took me to concerts and lectures and never made them seem stuffy or pretentious. He was constantly with beautiful and exciting women. I remember once passing through his bedroom on the way to the john and seeing a huge box next to his bed filled with what must have been a gross of condoms. My God! Did he really need that many?

And he cooked. Not brilliantly, but with panache. As with everything else, he enjoyed the process. For the first time, it occurred to me that cooking was more than just turning groceries into food. The act of cooking was a way to clear your mind and reacquaint yourself with your senses. Cooking involved not just the pleasure of eating good food but the pleasure of creating it as well. I was learning about the art of acting and the art of cooking and the art of living all at the same time.

Philip would invite me and a few friends up on a Sunday afternoon to shop and cook dinner. We threw together a simple spaghetti sauce, a quick sauté of onions, garlic, mushrooms, hamburger, tomatoes, and spices — nothing complicated, but lovingly chopped and sautéed and tasted by yours truly.

Then Philip taught me how to determine when spaghetti was perfectly done. He lifted a strand from the pot with a fork and flipped it against the wall behind the stove about two feet below the ceiling. If it stuck, the pasta was perfect. If it slithered down the wall, wait a few minutes more. His kitchen was decorated with dried strands of spaghetti all over the wall. Sort of like a Jackson Pollock. It wasn't until years later that I figured out that it works better to just taste the strand of spaghetti. Not as dramatic, but a hell of a lot more effective.

Philip's schoolboy sauce with its bargain-basement ingredients is a staple in my repertoire to this day — in the following two somewhat more sophisticated forms.

Beach House Pasta

Serves 8

Jill and I shared a beach house for six or so summers with a group of friends we still see today: Bruce Weitz and Ceci Hart, Marc and Mary Flanagan, Donny Scardino and Lizzie Lathram, Mary Beth Hurt and Victor Garber. They've all split up with their mates and gone on to other marriages and relationships, but I think the one thing that could bring them together in a spirit of harmony and tranquillity would be a gigantic bowl of beach house pasta. This is Philip's sauce — fifteen years later.

2 whole bulbs garlic
1 tablespoon butter
1 tablespoon olive oil, plus extra for sautéing
sugar
6 sweet red peppers
3/4 pound hot Italian sausage
3/4 pound sweet Italian sausage
4 strips thick-cut bacon
2 large yellow onions, chopped

1 pound lean ground chuck
2 28-ounce cans imported San Marzano tomatoes
salt and freshly ground black pepper
fresh basil leaves, chopped
crushed red pepper flakes
freshly grated Parmesan cheese

Preheat the oven to 200 degrees.

Chop 6 cloves of the garlic. Use the rest of the cloves to make roasted garlic pearls, or "nuggets of heaven," as I like to call them. Put the unpeeled cloves into boiling water for 3 minutes. Drain and peel them; then toss them in the combined butter and olive oil in an ovenproof dish or small sauté pan. Sprinkle a little sugar over them and place the pan in the preheated oven for a couple of hours, shaking carefully every now and then.

Blacken the red peppers by holding them on a fork and turning them over a gas or electric burner. Place them in a paper bag and close tightly.

Remove the sausage from its casing. Cut up the bacon into 1-inch squares.

Sauté the bacon and onions in a little olive oil in a large cast-iron skillet. Raise the heat and add the sausage meat in little bits. Add the ground chuck. As the meat browns, add half of the chopped garlic. When the meat is cooked through, add the canned tomatoes and their juice, stir, and lower the heat to a lively simmer. Add salt and black pepper to taste.

Meanwhile, remove the red peppers from the bag and peel off the blackened skins. Remove the seeds and ribs, cut the peppers into 1-inch squares, and add to the sauce.

Check the roasting garlic. It should be softening but not overbrowning.

After the sauce has simmered for about 45 minutes, add the roasted garlic, the rest of the raw, chopped garlic, some chopped fresh basil leaves, and the crushed red pepper. Taste for salt. The sauce now has garlic in three different forms — chopped and sautéed, roasted, and raw.

I recommend a large, comfortably chewy pasta such as rigatoni for this sauce. Cook it al dente — restrain yourself from flinging it against the wall — and drain it. Put it in a large bowl with a little sauce and grated fresh Parmesan. Toss to moisten the pasta. Bring the rest of the sauce to the table in another bowl — be sure to keep it hot — and serve cheese at the table as well.

Classic Bolognese Meat Sauce

Serves 8

There is no real connection between this authentically Italian sauce and the bastardized sauce above. But this one also has become a standard in my kitchen. I've synthesized it from a few different recipes — hats off to Marcella Hazan, Giulliano Buggialli, and Giorgio Baldi, the best Italian cook in Los Angeles. I make it in fairly large batches so I can freeze some in individual bags and heat it up when my psyche needs settling. Serve it over fresh fettuccine or, better yet, fresh tortellini. Top with cheese.

4 tablespoons olive oil	4 ounces pancetta,
4 tablespoons butter	finely chopped
1 large yellow onion	1 pound ground chuck
3 stalks celery with	1 pound ground veal
leaves	salt and freshly ground
3 carrots	pepper

2 cups dry white wine
1 cup milk
nutmeg

6 cups canned toma-
toes, drained

Heat the oil and butter in a heavy, deep pot. Finely chop the onion, celery, and carrots and sauté them until just cooked. Add the pancetta and cook for a few more minutes, then the ground chuck and veal, salt, and pepper and cook gently until the meat has just lost its color. Add the wine and cook until evaporated. Turn the heat down, add the milk and some freshly grated nutmeg. Let the milk evaporate. Add the tomatoes, stir, and let simmer for a few hours, stirring.

৵

Crumbs from a First Marriage

⤳ The very nature of a previous marriage implies a few errors in judgment, so I approach the memories of my early marital chutes and ladders . . . gingerly. I want to look and I don't want to look, if you know what I mean. But as I shake the tablecloth and watch the crumbs fall out, there are a few tasty morsels worth savoring again.

I imagine that Liz would say that I was the biggest crumb to come out of the whole situation, but I'm sure that now, with the passage of so much time and the wedding of our daughter behind us, she'd be happy to join me in looking back and having a few laughs. I could, of course, be wrong about that.

Let me begin with a disclosure that I've held heavily in my heart for the last twenty-seven years: the first dinner she ever cooked for me was bad. It was very, very bad. There, I've said it; it feels positively cathartic to finally blurt it out and be done with it. It was meat and it was gray — in the English tradition. I know that's a terrible generalization and English cuisine (the very phrase sticks in one's craw) has seen a renaissance in the past decade or so, but I'm going back some twenty-five years, when English cooking was English cooking. They were the only people in the world who could take vegetables fresh from the garden and in the wink of an eye make them taste canned. Liz came from that noble tradition. I should mention that she was English. Still is, although she's lived away from the Isle of Gray Meat long enough to have become quite proficient in the kitchen. But in those days she served up meals in the style of a school nutritionist. I was to receive a balanced diet, filled with all the right vitamins and things, and I would slowly die of acute sensory deprivation.

Now, you may well ask why I didn't cook the meals myself if I was such a hotshot in the kitchen, but this was 1967; we were still on the dark side of the movement that was about to shed its light on the world, and any wife worth her pillar of salt cooked for her husband. It's not that I didn't *want* to cook, you understand. But I deferred my desires in favor of her needs. I stepped back in gallant fashion to allow my new wife the space to express herself in the time-honored tradition of her sex. You buy that?

Stewed lamb chops and prunes, I think that first meal was. I smiled gratefully at my blushing bride and tucked into my dinner with husbandly gusto. Inside, my mind was racing. I was in a cold panic. I had to act quickly and decisively before a tradition was established and the light of pleasure would be forever extinguished from my life.

"Let's go out for dinner tomorrow night," I offered romantically. "You're working hard and you really deserve a special treat." She beamed. We went out for dinner every night for the rest of the year.

I bought cookbooks to slowly open up the possibilities of other cuisines, other cultures. I thought it would be good for her to see that the French, the Chinese, the Italians, thought of food as one of life's pleasures, as the focal point of gratification and well-being in an otherwise turbulent day and not merely as an unavoidable step in the daily digestive-eliminative process.

I started with the basics. The *Joy of Cooking,* the *New York Times Cookbook,* and Julia Child's *Mastering the Art of French Cooking.* And it worked; Liz became interested. I, however, became obsessed. I read them cover to cover as if they were novels. I discovered I had an innate sense of which recipes would please me in the eventual cooking and which were dismissable. I homed in on the mystery of the melding of taste and texture; texture is what hits the senses first, and taste is what lingers in the memory. Add in the bubbling expectations from the cooking aromas and you have anticipation, experience, and retrospection all stirred together in the same bite. That's what I call a good recipe. I searched these out and cooked them and cooked them until I owned them. I spent weeks and crates of eggs perfecting my omelet technique under the direction of the divine Julia. I practiced and perfected dishes such as coq au vin, boeuf bourguignonne, and carbonnade à la Flamande, all classics for the budding food snob that I was fast becoming. "Anything with booze in it," was my motto for a while.

I read with fascination about Napoleon and his chef, Dunand, on the battlefield of Marengo. It seems Napoleon never liked to eat before a battle — just like me, I thought! I like to wait until all the battles of the day are finished before I let my mind and my soul and my stomach relax and indulge themselves in a much-deserved reward for having faced the rigors of another day. Well, Napoleon, it seems, had battled himself far from his supply wagon, and Dunand was forced to improvise with what he could scrounge from the local farmers — three eggs, four tomatoes, six crayfish, a small hen, a little garlic, some oil, and a sauté pan, according to the *Larousse Gastronomique*. Thank God for local farmers — I'd be hard-pressed to do that well at my local Grand Union. Anyway, he browned the chicken in the oil, then fried the eggs in it, added the tomatoes and garlic and some brandy from the general's flask, and put the crayfish on top to steam. Napoleon was delighted and no doubt gave Dunand Austria or some other small country to play with for feeding him so well that day. Now, I have cooked chicken Marengo many times over the years. Judging from the stains on my cookbook, I have cooked it more than any other battle dish in my repertoire, but usually in the modern way, substituting mushrooms for crayfish and white wine for brandy, and cooking it in my kitchen instead of on a battlefield.

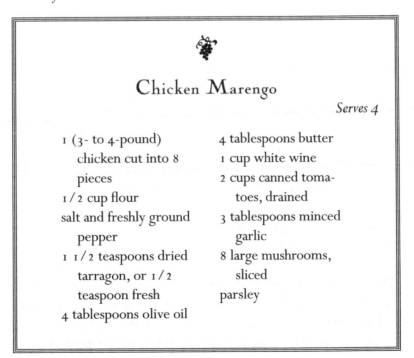

Chicken Marengo

Serves 4

1 (3- to 4-pound) chicken cut into 8 pieces	4 tablespoons butter
	1 cup white wine
	2 cups canned toma-
1/2 cup flour	toes, drained
salt and freshly ground pepper	3 tablespoons minced garlic
1 1/2 teaspoons dried tarragon, or 1/2 teaspoon fresh	8 large mushrooms, sliced
	parsley
4 tablespoons olive oil	

Preheat the oven to 350 degrees.

Dredge the chicken in the flour, salt, pepper, and tarragon. Press the flour into the skin of the chicken pieces and shake the excess back onto the plate.

Brown the chicken pieces in the oil and butter.

When it is thoroughly browned, remove the chicken to an enameled cast-iron pot or other ovenproof pot.

Pour the remaining seasoned flour from the plate into the remaining hot fat in the skillet and whisk to make a roux. Brown to a dark gold, then whisk in the wine a little at a time.

Put the tomatoes, garlic, and mushrooms over and around the chicken pieces, then pour the sauce over.

Cover the pot tightly and bake about 45 minutes. Sprinkle with the parsley and serve.

Some friend had given us Roy Andries de Groot's *Feast for All Seasons* as a wedding present, and it served as a virtual primer for me. Now that I had established myself — in my mind — as a culinary prodigy, I used de Groot's book to ingest all the world's gastronomy in one swallow. In one typical week, I jumped from Chinese Chow Bow (abalone with vegetables) to Indian Tali Machi (gray sole in spiced batter) to Greek Stefado of Beef. I had become an international terrorist in the kitchen.

This book, with its shopping and cooking hints, its vast range of recipes, and its arrogant insistence on doing things the right way and only the right way became a favorite with Liz and me, and we cooked and learned a great deal from it. From the year in New Haven where we met and married, to the three years in

Milwaukee, where Alison was born, to the years in D.C., where the marriage finally ended, we studiously stained the pages of de Groot. It became the focus of a major custody battle in the end. I got it, but I had to give up the house in exchange. A fair deal, all in all. Here's my somewhat simplified version of a favorite from it.

Shrimp with Sauce Rémoulade

Serves 4

I've made this piquant little dish many times — most notably when Bob Benedetti and I offered to cater a friend's wedding for 150 people in Milwaukee. Bob was a director at the Rep and a prodigious gourmand — and just as impetuous a fool as I was. We realized the insanity of our endeavor two nights before the wedding as we watched the dawn breaking halfway through the shelling of more shrimp than I ever want to see again. However, we persevered and cooked an enormously successful banquet — much more successful than the marriage turned out to be.

This entire dish must be prepared the day before.

1 to 2 cups dry white wine	3 stalks celery with leaves, chopped
1 to 2 cups tarragon white wine vinegar	2 cloves garlic, slivered
1 to 2 cups cold water	2 bay leaves

salt and freshly ground black pepper	24 jumbo shrimps Sauce Rémoulade
cayenne	(see following recipe)

In a large saucepan, add a cup each of the wine, vinegar, and cold water. Add the garlic, bay leaves, celery, salt, pepper, and a dash of cayenne. Bring the mixture to a boil and simmer for a half hour or so.

Meanwhile, wash the shrimps, remove the legs, but do not shell. When the brew has simmered, drop them in, adding more wine, vinegar, and water in equal parts if needed to cover. Return to a boil and then time for 5 minutes if the shrimps are really large — if not, 3 minutes will do. Turn off the heat and let them cool to room temperature. Refrigerate in the liquid for 24 hours. Prepare the sauce.

Sauce Rémoulade

Makes about one cup

3 or 4 sprigs parsley	4 tablespoons spicy
1 / 2 heart white celery	mustard Hungarian sweet red
1 small red onion	paprika
2 tablespoons sherry vinegar	salt and freshly ground pepper
6 tablespoons olive oil	1 bunch watercress

Chop very finely the parsley, celery heart, and onion. Mix them in a bowl with the vinegar, olive oil, mustard, paprika, and rather more salt and pepper than usual. Put the mixture in a tightly sealed jar and refrigerate overnight.

Next day, several hours before the dish is to be served, shell the shrimps. Mix the shrimps with the rémoulade and leave in the refrigerator at least two hours. Serve on chopped watercress.

Liz's father gave us a most wonderful wedding present. In the summer following our first year together, he brought us over to England and treated us to a two-month honeymoon traveling around Europe. We had bought a little powder-blue Sunbeam Alpine sports car that we picked up in London on the overseas delivery plan, which allowed us to drive it around Europe for a few months, then ship it home as a used car. I don't think I have ever been so excited — my first new car, my first sports car, my first major purchase on an installment plan! I had cleaned out our paltry savings account for the down payment and hocked the next three years of our future to pay for it, but this sleek little two-seater roadster was mine, and all the roads of Europe lay before me with no speed limits to hold me back. I was Mr. Toad personified.

I half listened as the salesman in the Piccadilly Circus dealership went over the fine points of the car. I was bleary-eyed from a night of travel and too excited to concentrate. I figured I'd read the manual later when I had time. He deftly displayed how to take the top down, which I took no notice of, and we were on our way.

It seemed that ours was the only car in London with left-hand drive and I was the only driver with a penchant for driving on the other side of the road. I pulled out of the dealership parking garage and almost plowed head-on into a taxi. I threw up my arms in apology as every car in central London blew its horn at me. I backed up, apologized again, and got myself to the proper side of the road. It started to drizzle.

"I think we should put the top up," Liz said gently as I turned the wrong way into a roundabout and faced hundreds of honking cars all coming in the opposite direction. I had been in this situation before in a bumper-car ride at Gwynn Oak Amusement Park in 1953 and I knew I had to get turned around as quickly as possible. The rain got heavier.

"Perhaps I could put it up while you drive," she said. I was too busy to reply.

If only I could get north to the suburbs, I could find a place to pull over and get things together, but no matter what I did, I ended up heading south back to the center of London. Liz was reading the soaking-wet map and directing me with that steady, low-key English cadence that she hoped would inspire calm. I was seconds away from throttling her. After the third screeching near-accident, where a man in a Jaguar sedan bellowed horrible obscenities at me in a charming North Country accent, I spied a gas station and managed to pull in for sanctuary. The owner was an older man wearing a mackintosh. He leaned down with both forearms resting on my door and gazed at me and my brand spanking new, left-hand drive, sopping-wet sports car for a long moment.

"You should get that top up," he said cheerfully. The three of us managed to do that and then mop up the puddles on the floor.

"Come in and have a cup of tea," he said. "You need it."

We did and it worked its magic. We sipped our tea. The sun

came out. He gave me secret plans, which I wrote down carefully, on how to escape London. We had a second cup, which he insisted I needed, and a biscuit or two. We discussed the weather, which was, indeed, changeable, and then he and I practiced putting up my convertible top a few times just to make sure I didn't get caught out.

Liz and I spent a week in Duxford, a tiny village a few miles outside of Cambridge, where I met the family and experienced firsthand the source of Liz's English cooking instincts. My heart yearned for Europe, my car veered instinctually for the other side of the road, my palate insisted on a break from bangers and mash, so soon we were off.

We took the ferry from Harwich to the Hook of Holland and drove to The Hague for our first night. My first taste of Europe remains one of the best to this day. A little broodjes shop offered up sandwiches on the softest, freshest rolls I have ever tasted. Roast beef with butter, salt, and pepper was my choice. I had never experienced farm-fresh butter before and it was a life-changing event. Perhaps this was where I started to learn that simple and fresh is an unbeatable combination and that ornate and saucy only came into being when the former was unavailable.

Then we drove to Amsterdam. It was packed with young, long-haired, drugged-out kids from all over the world. The city vibrated with energy. The primary mode of transportation was two-wheeled — mopeds and bicycles. They were everywhere. My sports car suddenly felt too big and middle-class, so we parked in the center of town and set off to reconnoiter on foot. In cafés that spilled out onto the streets we joined hippies and college kids dressed like hippies as they sat in the glorious hot sun and guzzled Dutch beer and genever, an aromatic local gin; it was Fort Lauderdale with an accent. We consulted our Frommer's *Europe on Five Dollars a Day* to find ourselves a good, cheap bed-and-breakfast, but the city was packed. For a while it seemed that we wouldn't find any place to stay, as we climbed the steep front steps of one hotel after the other only to be told there were no vacancies. As we turned away from the last one on our list, the concierge called me back.

"You are a Jew," she said in Yiddish.

Although I was in no way fluent in the language, that phrase was easy to comprehend. I nodded yes. I couldn't tell from her manner whether she was hostile or friendly.

"From where are you from?"

"America."

"No, before that," she said.

"My grandparents are from Lithuania."

"Come in," and she waved at us to follow her. We waited in the small foyer while she made a phone call. She spoke animatedly for a long time, then she hung up.

"I am speaking to a man who was very important in the Resistance," she said. "We worked together during the occupation. He is seeing whether he has any room for you in his hotel."

While we waited, she told us a story of a group of Amsterdamers who risked their lives to save their Jewish neighbors during the war. She had been a food smuggler. She bicycled out to the countryside, where she could buy extra provisions without arousing suspicion, then stuffed the contraband breads and smoked meats under her clothes and waited until dark to bring it to the Jews who were hiding in attics and basements throughout the city. Her son had been a student at the local polytechnic who became an explosives expert for the freedom fighters. When she told us of his execution at the hands of the Nazis, there was no sadness in her face, only pride and love.

Her friend had no room at his hotel but gave us the name and address of a woman who took in boarders in a suburb of the city. She too had been in the Resistance; she too had lost a son as well as her husband to the Nazis. We moved into a large, airy bedroom in her apartment. We had to take the bus into town every day, and perhaps we gave up a little privacy, but we gained an intimacy with the city that no hotel would have given us. She was formal at first when she served us breakfast, but after a few days she joined us at the table and shared memories with us. A Dutch breakfast is a formidable affair with a huge assortment of cheeses, cold meats, eggs, and breads, and we spent a good hour every morning getting to know each other. A hero — or heroine, in this case — is just a regular person, it seems, who responds intuitively in remarkable circumstances. She had no concept of having done anything extraordinary, only that people she loved had been murdered and that time had gone very slowly since then.

After Amsterdam was Brussels and my first taste of moules marinière. They were everywhere! At first we didn't realize what they were advertising at every bistro we passed, because the signs just announced Les Spécialités! What this meant was that it was mussel season in Belgium, a yearly event that has the national significance of the Fourth of July, at least. We stopped at a bistro that had tables outside and watched the passing scene while downing bowls full of mussels, the shells piling up precariously in the center of the table. But the best part for me — even better than the sweet, tender mussels themselves — was breaking off chunks of crusty bread and sopping up the wonderful wine-and-herb-scented mussel broth in the bottom of the tureen.

Moules Marinière

Serves 6

Figure a quart of mussels per person; then throw in an extra half-quart or so for good measure.

6 to 7 quarts mussels	1 / 2 teaspoon thyme
6 to 8 shallots, minced	6 tablespoons butter
3 to 4 sprigs parsley	2 glasses dry white
1 bay leaf	wine

First and foremost, scrub the mussels. Then pull off the beard, which will give you a little tug-of-war. Then soak the mussels in water for an hour or two, adding a little flour to the water to help them clean themselves of sand. Then wash and drain them again.

Put the mussels in a large, heavy pot with all the rest of the ingredients, cover tightly, and boil. Shake the pot briskly every now and then. After 5 minutes or so of boiling they should be done. Make sure all the shells have opened. If any have not, discard them. Shovel the mussels into soup plates, pour some broth over the top, and go to town. Don't forget the bread and some cold white wine.

Right about the time we hit Germany, my Sunbeam passed six hundred miles on the odometer, and according to the manual I could finally open it up full throttle. I had been waiting for this moment. I cruised up the entrance ramp to the autobahn, checked my rearview mirror, and floored it. I red-lined it in second and eased it into third. My engine had that great, throaty sports car sound as I ran it through the gears. When I dropped it into high gear, I just let it fly; and as I watched the speedometer arcing over ninety miles per hour and felt that flush of speed and power that validated my manhood, a big black Mercedes sedan silently swooshed by me as if I were going thirty. I never saw it coming; it was on me and by me before you could say Fahrvergnügen. My little blue sports car felt exactly like what it was — little and blue. I dropped it down to a safe, middle-class sixty five, pointed it south, and didn't stop until I was in Switzerland.

Switzerland itself left me feeling kind of neutral. I don't have many vibrant memories. I had planned for months to find Charlie Chaplin's house in Vevey and stop in to pay my respects and have him recognize my genius and pronounce me his spiritual heir, but when we got close, I decided to leave him alone. The best thing Switzerland did for me was to get me to France, where I have surely lived before in any number of lives and hope to live again in this one.

Our first stop was a splurge — a real hotel instead of a bed-and-breakfast. It was perched on a mountainside somewhere between Annecy and Chambéry, and if memory serves, it was aptly named l'Hôtel Eden. I experienced my first French meal, and it remains one of the best I've ever had. Pike quenelles in lobster sauce, mustardy green salad, freshly made baguettes — I remember those courses vividly; the rest of the meal has faded away. The quenelles were an epiphany for me — especially after all that German and Swiss food. It had never occurred to me that a taste could be subtle and powerful at the same time — delicate, yet intensely memorable.

We left Eden — in many ways never to return — and headed south. We had bouillabaisse in Marseilles overlooking the harbor as we were supposed to and gave money to a black woman carrying her white baby because she roused our social conscience, until we saw her partner — a white woman with a black baby — working the other side of the street.

At this point we had to decide whether to go left to Italy or right to Spain. We had been invited to Formentera, an island off the coast of Barcelona, by an old school chum of mine known as Psychedelic Billy. He was there avoiding the draft and taking advantage of the drug trade from northern Africa. So we headed to Spain, leaving Italy for another time. Destiny was saving this great treasure for me until I was ready, and that was to be many years later in what seemed to be a different life, with what was certainly a different wife.

Spain disappeared in a marijuana blur. The island had no electricity and only a little propane gas, so we lived on tortillas, beer, and illegal substances. I do remember we were running out of money, so we stayed there for a couple of weeks, as it cost almost nothing.

The most perfect moment I remember from Spain actually happened in France. We drove straight from Barcelona, where our car had been parked, to the French border. The heat was blistering and we were parched and sunburned — the top was stuck down again. And then, just as we cleared the French border, there was a little fruit stand on the side of the road selling fresh peaches. They were big and perfectly ripe and looked as if they had been picked by Cézanne. We bought six of them, parked the car on the side of the road, and plunged in. The juice was so plentiful it seemed to explode out of the fruit. Peach juice dripped off our fingers, ran down our chins, and permeated the black leather upholstery of the Sunbeam. It leaped into our parched mouths and quenched our thirst with its sweet, liquid-gold, faintly tart wetness. We couldn't stop eating. And dripping. And laughing at how good they were. We had our best moment of the trip there in the dry countryside with the wet peaches. One of the best moments we ever had.

Oh, yes, I remember another great moment. Two years later, in Milwaukee, we were waiting for the birth of our daughter, who was almost two weeks late. I did what I have often done in crises. I went out and bought two hoagies with lots of onions and hot peppers and enough olive oil to help them slide down easily, and brought them back for us to munch on while waiting for dilation. Liz couldn't have been more than two bites into hers when all hell broke loose. Alison was born much later that night — I'd like to say she came out clutching a pimiento, but it wouldn't be true. So here, without FDA approval, is what became known as the Labor-Inducing Hoagie.

Labor-Inducing Hoagie

Start with the freshest loaf of Italian bread you can find — or even better, bake it yourself.

1 hoagie-size loaf of bread per person	thin slices of imported ham, salami, capacola,
olive oil and red wine vinegar vinaigrette	mortadella, provolone cheese, American cheese

iceberg lettuce,
shredded
ripe tomato, sliced
very thin
yellow onions, thinly
shredded

oregano
cherry peppers or
jalapeños, seeded
and chopped
(optional)

Slice the bread lengthwise and soak both halves with a good dose of the vinaigrette. Dole out the meats and cheeses liberally, pile on the lettuce, tomato, and onion, pour on more vinaigrette, sprinkle oregano over all; hot peppers optional. Serve at once.

The next evening I went straight from the hospital to the theater, where we were performing *Midsummer Night's Dream*. I had spent the day with my newborn daughter. I had counted her fingers and toes and looked for blemishes as all fathers must do and was satisfied that she was flawless. It wasn't until the trauma of the birth was over and we were past any danger that I allowed myself to realize how much anxiety I had been suppressing. And at the end of the show that night, standing offstage waiting for the curtain call, I listened for what must have been the hundredth time to Oberon's benediction to the wedding couples. But it was the first time I really heard the words:

Never mole, hare-lip, nor scar,
Nor mark prodigious, such as are
Despised in nativity,
Shall upon their children be.

And I started to cry — in happiness and in wonder, for I knew I had witnessed a miracle: that a perfect child could be born from two such imperfect people.

So when I look back at the foibles of my first marriage, I don't think of it as time lost, or love squandered, or commitment gone awry. It happened for a reason. A baby was born with a personality as vibrant and mysterious as a glittering ruby; an old soul came back around who, as I watch her even now, is still in the process of discovering how much she knows. I feel lucky that I get the chance to watch.

Jill

She was sitting on the kitchen floor with her legs tucked under, listening to the theater's chief electrician play the guitar and sing country music. It was 1970 and she was wearing a miniskirt. I couldn't pull my eyes away. I tried to be cool. I kept leaving the room, only to drift back in to catch her at another angle. Her endless blue eyes, the serene perfection of her features, the secrets barely hidden by her miniskirt — all pulled me toward her. They pull me still . . . but I'm getting ahead of myself.

Liz and I, with eight-month-old Alison in tow, packed up and left Milwaukee. I drove a Toyota sedan, having traded in my sports car for something more sensible. We were on our way to New York so that I could have my inevitable confrontation with the commercial theater. I was scared. I had been in the protective atmosphere of the Milwaukee Repertory Theater for three seasons and felt very much at home there. I had acted in more than twenty plays, rehearsing one during the day while performing another at night. Shakespeare, Shaw, and Chekhov;

Williams, Wilder, and Becket; it was actor heaven. It was my baptism by fire. I had no time to question whether I could act, I just got out there every night and did it. And when the three seasons were over, I looked around and realized that I had become an actor.

I had a steady income, a wife, a daughter, and a job as long as I wanted it. And I knew something was drastically wrong. I felt like a civil-service worker. This was not the life I had in mind for myself. Where was the excitement, the danger, the feeling of performing on the high wire without a net? Regional theater was a good-enough training ground, but unless I moved on, I would bore myself to death. I told Liz that I had decided to go to New York and try my luck — with no prospects, no connections, and no visible means of support. She looked at me as if she suddenly didn't know who I was. After all, I was throwing away her security along with my own. But I was adamant. So she gamely said good-bye to her friends, clutched her baby to her breast, and helped me pack the car. What choice did she have?

I found a sublet apartment that was advertised on the bulletin board at Actor's Equity in New York. It was a fourth-floor walk-up in Yorkville, a German immigrant neighborhood on the Upper East Side of Manhattan. The apartment was small and hot, and when Liz found Alison happily playing with a cockroach in her playpen, she decided this was no place for a baby. She took her down to Baltimore and stayed with my parents while I searched for a job in New York. Living with my parents was not Liz's idea of heaven, but at least she and the baby would have air-conditioning until I figured out what I was doing with my life. It wasn't a perfect solution, but this was not a perfect time.

I got a job. It was off-off-Broadway, a workshop production of a new play at the Truck and Warehouse Theater in the East

Village. I thought the play was terrible. I had just finished doing *The Three Sisters* in Milwaukee and was a complete snob about the theater. I didn't realize then that in the years to come I would be very happy to get a job like that.

After rehearsals I roamed the streets of New York. I was alone, without a family, working for nothing in a play I couldn't stand, broke, filled with guilt, confused about the future; I was an actor.

Then fate interceded, in the guise of Rosemary Tischler. Rosemary headed the casting office of TCG (Theater Communications Group), which was a clearing house for all the regional theaters in the country. She had always been very supportive of me and had followed my career in Milwaukee. Now she had an offer for me to join the company at Arena Stage in Washington, D.C. Arena was considered the most prestigious regional theater in the country, and I had always aspired to work there. Needless to say, Liz and my parents were in favor of it, so I buckled. I gave notice on the play in New York and headed back to the relative safety of regional theater. I was uneasy about the decision. I was going backward, or sideways at best. I knew it was time for me to face New York and that I was copping out.

At the same time all this was going on, Rosemary was also encouraging a young actress, fresh from Yale drama school, to accept an offer for a season at Arena Stage. Her name was Jill Eikenberry.

So when I fixated on Jill sitting on the kitchen floor that night in Washington, I knew I was out of line. I shouldn't even have been looking, but some decisions are made in places other than the mind and this was one of them. She was almost engaged to a college sweetheart who lived in Montreal. I was married and had a kid. So in the following weeks, when I held forth in the greenroom about art and the true meaning of life (subjects bound to capture the attention of young ingenues coming out of drama school) and watched her eyes shining up at me with unabashed adoration, I had no idea that destiny was shifting under my feet. I thought I was in charge — a harmless sexual tease, an ego boost, a simple dalliance, at the worst — I couldn't see that I was flying at the speed of light out of the life I knew and into an unknown future.

We went out for drinks every night after the show — always in the company of other friends. We stared into each other's eyes across the table, but that was all. Not a finger, your honor. We could have sworn in a court of law that we were innocent — even though we knew in our hearts we were guilty as hell. And then, during rehearsals for *Mother Courage,* the second show of the season, we took the fateful step. It was me, really. She was about to go to Montreal for the weekend to visit her fiancé, and I insisted that we consummate the relationship before she went. She wanted to wait at least until she got back. I knew if we waited, it would never happen. I won.

We then entered what could be referred to as the cheese-steak chapter of our relationship. For those of you who aren't familiar with this delectable, diet-busting goodie, I'll explain. A cheese-steak is a sandwich, a big sandwich, that originated in Philadelphia, if you believe local lore. It's served on a submarine roll, also known as a hoagie or grinder, and contains paper-thin sliced steak thrown onto a hot griddle with onions and sautéed in olive oil. A little mozzarella cheese is melted over the whole concoction, which is then lifted onto a warm roll and covered with tomato sauce, salt, and pepper — and a few hot peppers, if you go that way. Actually, a classic cheese-steak has no sauce, but I always thought it was a nice addition. If you want to make this at home (and you should), partially freeze the steak before you slice it. It's much easier.

Now, the way this sandwich fit into my romantic life is a sor-
did tale that mixes some of the worst aspects of lust and glut-
tony, although I've always been hard put to tell the two apart.
Every night, when the performance was over, Jill and I went
back to her bachelorette apartment and spent part of the night
together. Then at about two in the morning I crept out to my
car and started the long guilty trip home. But on the way I
stopped at a sleazy little sandwich shop — it was the only thing
open at that hour. I hauled my equally sleazy conscience up onto
a stool, munched on a cheese-steak, and tried to sort out my
miserable life. I don't think I've ever been as hungry as I was on
that stool every night. I could have eaten two — even three —
of those huge sandwiches. Some nights I did. The counterman,
an older black man who looked as if he had seen it all, couldn't
figure out this odd, lonely character across the counter from
him — this middle-class Jewish boy showing up like clockwork
at two in the morning with a perturbed look on his face, Max
Factor pancake makeup all around his collar, and an insatiable
appetite for cheese-steaks with tomato sauce and hot peppers.
I've always wondered if that incredible hunger was a metaphor,
whether I was trying to fill some emptiness in my soul, or hide
the ache of my guilt — or whether the entire affair with Jill
was just an excuse to get out of the house to eat cheese-steaks
with impunity at two in the morning.

The affair bumped along inexorably toward the end of the
season. We were in love and we were in pain, and we didn't
know how to get out of either one. We knew that what we were
doing was wrong; we just couldn't stop it. And everyone —
with the exception of my wife — knew about it. At the theater,
our friends would flash embarrassed, understanding smiles at us
as we passed in the halls. And the routine of sneaking off to Jill's
apartment every night and every afternoon we were free from

rehearsal was starting to pale. We were outlaws. And whereas that added a lot of spice to the proceedings, we were becoming increasingly aware that it also deprived us of certain luxuries necessary to the development of a relationship. Time, for example. We had to cram every ounce of our energies for each other into the short interludes we could steal. There was no time for breathing space between. And we also felt cheated out of spending the whole night together. Cheese-steaks notwithstanding, I was losing patience with the kind of intimus interruptus that we had to go through every night. We were being robbed of that special moment of quiet reflection — call it afterglow or snuggling — when she feels the continuing glow of passion slowly ebbing away, and he falls into a deep, instant, snoring sleep. We couldn't allow ourselves that. What if we fell asleep, not to wake up until morning? Then the whole intrigue would come crashing down around us — a possibility we both dreaded and craved.

Then came a memorable meal that altered the course of our relationship. This was a dinner cooked by Jill — I think the last one she ever cooked — and I wasn't even invited. She was cooking for the parents of some friends from Yale. They lived in the area and were coming to the show that night. In the process of preparing moussaka, she missed the eggplant with her paring knife and plunged it into the fleshy part of her hand, between the thumb and first finger. Was this merely culinary ineptitude, or was it a desperate signal to me that our affair couldn't go on like this any longer? The fact was we were both getting a little nuts. Jill was pounding her fists on the wall of her apartment every night in frustration over our situation. And I was taking it out on Liz, who had no idea what was going on, or if she did, wasn't admitting it to herself. I would pick fights with her, venting all my frustration and guilt and rage, because I couldn't face the truth. I couldn't admit to myself that I wanted to leave.

So Jill arrived at the theater that night with her hand all bandaged, and by the end of the show it was clear that it wouldn't stop bleeding. I decided that she had to see a doctor.

We went to the emergency room of the nearest hospital, which was one of those huge, urban factories with ambulances flying in and out, and we were told to wait in a long hallway with all the other patients. There had just been a three-car accident, so the hallway was packed with people in various stages of medical emergency. We sat there in the unreal glow of the fluorescent light bouncing off the sickly green hospital walls; we listened to the soft moans of the accident victims, and we waited.

Suddenly, far off down the hallway, there appeared a little, wizened Indian gentleman, bearing a striking resemblance to Mahatma Gandhi, running for all he was worth to get out of the hospital. He was naked except for a hospital sheet hastily pulled around him. Three orderlies were in hot pursuit. He disappeared out one door, only to pop in again through another door closer to us. And always the orderlies were about ten steps behind him. We — Jill and I and all the accident victims — started to laugh. It was like watching a Marx Brothers movie, but even more bizarre. Sometimes he would dart across the hall very close to us, and then, seconds later, he would be hundreds of yards up the hallway. And each time he shot out, we all would shout encouragement. We wanted him to get away. He symbolized the panic we all felt that night. We all wanted to get away.

Hours later, after Jill's hand was treated and properly bandaged, I drove her back to her apartment. We sat in the car and didn't speak. It was late; I had to get home. There was no time to make love. There was no time for cheese-steaks. We sat quietly for a long time. I knew I was hopelessly in love and there was no way back. This was no affair. This was the rest of our lives.

Once we admitted that, we began to crave legitimacy. We were fated. We were perfect together — synchronous and seamless — and being actors we wanted to show off our perfection to the largest audience possible. It was time to move this show out of the off-Broadway basement and onto the Great White Way. Bob Prosky, who at that time was the reigning character actor and resident sage at the theater, sensed our predicament and suggested privately to me that perhaps I needed to get away — if only for a night or two — to think things over, to get perspective, to spend a blessed night with this woman to see if we could still bear each other after waking up in the cold light of morning. He had a house in Cape May, New Jersey — still does, I'll wager — that he offered for the getaway. I lied, badly, to Liz about how I needed some solitude. It was clear that neither of us believed this story, but off I went anyway. It turned out that Bob's wife, Ida, and his two young sons would be there that weekend, and since we didn't want to stigmatize them with our sins, we booked a cheap little motel nearby. Cheap little motel. The words still have the power to rouse.

The night together was all it had been cracked up to be. And afterward we slept. How we slept! We slept and we slept and we slept. What a novelty! What bliss! We woke up, smiled at each other, and then slept some more. It had a profound effect on me. I still enjoy sleeping to this day.

When we finally broke the spell and got out of bed, we went to the cheap little motel's dining room to have our first breakfast together. The food was not memorable. Jill had the same breakfast that she was to have every morning for the next fifteen years — she can be a little set in her ways — one piece of toast, one boiled egg, one slice of American cheese, orange juice, no coffee. I gazed at her across the polyurethane table over my cup of weak coffee and my English muffin completely devoid of nooks, crannies, texture, and taste and realized that we had passed the point of no return. No return to subterfuge, no return to interruptus, no return to wife. We were out there, two desperadoes with nothing to lose and nothing in our bank account, but with the ever-increasing certainty of our love and the uncertain, tenuous belief in our talent. And as I think about it, that's really all we still have. We're older, we've had a lot of success, there's a bit more money in the bank, but the fact is, we're still out there — with just our love and talent to see us through, to take us to the next adventure.

SEVEN

New York

꘏

꘏ We arrived in New York in the winter of 1971. We must have seemed like a small band of refugees from a Third World country; at least we seemed that way to ourselves. We had Alison, who by mutual consent of all parties was to be brought up by Jill and me. And we had our baby-sitter, Mrs. Sutton, who had come to work for us in Washington when we were both busy at the theater and now consented to leave the District of Columbia for the first time in her life. We carried with us a few meager possessions: our bank account, which came to $350 between us; large bills from the divorce lawyers on both sides of the case, which I had agreed to pay in a burst of ill-advised generosity; and, praise the Lord, a job. Jill had been in a production of Michael Weller's *Moonchildren* in Washington, which was optioned by David Merrick to be produced on Broadway. I managed to land a tiny role and understudy chores, so we were going to be pulling down two salaries and working on Broadway. Not a bad way to start life in New York. My old buddy, Bruce Weitz, was working down in Washington, so he let us live in his New York apartment while we looked for a place of our own. We were on our way. Almost.

Mrs. Sutton took one look at the winos lying on the front steps of Bruce's East Fourth Street apartment and gave notice. We begged her to stay just until the show opened so that we would have time to find a replacement. Reluctantly, she agreed. Meanwhile we scouted for an apartment. Through ads in the *Village Voice,* I found a very charming fourth-floor walk-up on Perry Street in the heart of the West Village — one of the best neighborhoods in New York. It was a lot more than we wanted to spend, but fortunately the show had just opened to rave reviews and we were clearly going to be employed for a while. We grabbed the apartment, let poor Mrs. Sutton return to the more familiar dangers of southwest Washington, enrolled Alison in a day-care center, and were finally, actually, on our way. Almost.

The show closed. After only two weeks. We were outraged and confused; but mostly, we were broke. David Merrick apparently had his attention and his money tied up in *Sugar,* a musical, which was having troubles out of town. Left to its own devices, our wonderful little play was ignored, ran out of money, and closed. After the last performance, we packed up our makeup and opening-night telegrams that had been displayed so proudly on our mirrors, bundled up against the winter, which was getting colder by the minute, and trudged to the Forty-second Street subway to go home. Along Broadway we ran into Pierre Epstein, an actor we had known briefly down in Washington.

"I heard your show closed," he said. We nodded.

"Tough town," said Pierre, and he smiled and wended his way up Broadway.

We looked at each other, with the full weight of what was

facing us — no job, no prospects, no money, an apartment we couldn't afford, bills due to the day-care center and the lawyers, at least an eight-week wait for the unemployment insurance to kick in — and we started to laugh, a little hysterically, perhaps, but really just because Pierre's statement was so pretentious, so patronizing, and so well-timed. To this day, whenever things get a little rough, one of us will inevitably say to the other, "Tough town."

My part in *Moonchildren* had been so small — I had one line at the end of the play — that I had little hope of attracting interest from agents or producers. But, amazingly, a few days after we closed, I got a call from a commercial agent who said she had seen me in the play and got my number from Actor's Equity.

"Can you get to an audition this afternoon?" I couldn't believe she had noticed me in my tiny role, much less singled me out.

"I was the milkman, right? The one at the end?"

"Yeah, I know. Can you make it this afternoon?" I took down the address and the time of the audition.

There were hundreds of actors in the casting office, character types of every ethnic background. The commercial was for Ballantine beer. The idea was that they were sponsoring "the Ballantine Summer Games." They filmed highlights of street games like stickball and skin-the-cat and covered them as if they were Olympic events. And instead of athletes, the participants were regular New York guys with potbellies and receding hairlines. How could I miss?

Two days later the agent called and told me I had booked the job. I was to be the torchbearer. They filmed me running through New York in boxer shorts and a T-shirt carrying an Olympic torch. I ran past neighborhood bars and delis, past the piers downtown, past construction sites, through Times Square and Columbus Circle. We shot for fourteen hours. I had never run so far in my entire life. But I was exhilarated. This was my first movie experience, my first time in front of a camera. And whereas I knew this wasn't exactly like Dustin Hoffman getting that part in *The Graduate,* my imagination started to envision a chain of events that would lead me straight to Hollywood and a major movie contract. Someone would notice — someone big:

"Who's that guy with the torch?" "What a face!" "Find me that actor, the one in the shorts! He's perfect!"

Well, that didn't happen. The commercial ran briefly. I saw it only once, and I watched for it eighteen hours a day. Then the whole campaign folded. I called the agent and she said she would keep me in mind if there were any other calls for ethnic types. But that was it. The phone was silent.

I had time to explore the neighborhood — lots of time. Bleeker Street was right around the corner, and after I dropped Alison off at Child's Garden on Abington Square every morning, I would stroll along, window-shopping at the stores I couldn't afford, avoiding my apartment and my telephone, whose silence was a constant, stinging source of rejection. Bleeker Street became my toy store, my land of the sugarplum fairies. Pierre Deux had the antique French country furniture that I envisioned in my house; Aspidistra had the exotic plants that would enliven the rooms. And the food! Ottomanelli's butcher shop with its homemade sausages and perfectly sliced and pounded scallopini of veal. Zito's bakery, where I would indulge myself in a baguette every morning as I sipped my cup of take-out coffee from McNulty's on Christopher Street. Aphrodisia, a spice and tea shop with its little bottles and flasks and bins filled with every aroma from every corner of the world. And if I felt really adventurous, I would head for Sixth Avenue, where the *really* expensive food stores were: Balducci's, with its best of the best — produce, deli, cheese, prime meats, bread, and the finest packaged and bottled gourmet treats. It was an amusement park for gluttons. And the Jefferson market right up the street, a neighborhood market that catered to the million-dollar brownstones that sit between Fifth and Sixth Avenues in the West Village. Even though I couldn't afford anything fancy, I began to understand how New Yorkers shopped and cooked. It was more like Europe, in a sense. You bought what looked good and what you needed for that day. There was no car to carry bags and bags of groceries for the week, so you purchased what you could carry comfortably. And given that we lived in a fourth-floor walk-up, I tended to buy very small, very light portions of things. Also, New York kitchens were tiny — at least mine was — and there wasn't nearly as much room for storage as I was used to.

All these restrictions, budget being the uppermost, tested my cooking skills. And I think they made me a better cook in the long run. Sometimes, having parameters makes you focus more clearly on the work. I know it's that way in acting. Well, here my parameters were a tiny kitchen, a minuscule budget, and pressure to produce exciting, satisfying meals that were often the only bright spot in our day. What I had was lots of time and a tremendous need to put my creative energies to use. Cooking became my outlet, my solitary art, my loyal friend when no one else in New York would give me the time of day. And no one had to hire me to do it; no auditions were required. Alison and Jill were a captive audience, and they had to be there for the length of the run. So, while other actors hung around union halls or agents' offices or, worse yet, bars to pass the time between auditions, I had instead my ancient, mystical craft to practice. And it gave me everything — a challenge for my imagination, a sense of purpose and identity, a pathway to a meditative, almost Zen-like state, and, once a day, a satisfying meal to make us all feel full and stimulated and lucky to be alive. These were the days when I really learned to cook.

RECIPES FOR
OUT-OF-WORK ACTORS

The idea here is to take simple dishes with easily accessible and affordable ingredients and kick them up to another level by the method of cooking. The tomatoes and garlic in the first pasta recipe are enhanced by roasting them rather than the familiar sautéeing, and this brings a richer, deeper flavor to the dish.

Spaghetti with Roast Tomatoes and Garlic
Serves 4

10 Italian plum toma-
    toes
1 whole bulb garlic
1 / 2 cup olive oil
salt and freshly ground
    black pepper

1 pound spaghetti
crushed red pepper
    flakes
fresh basil, chopped
Parmesan cheese

Preheat the oven to 400 degrees.

Blanch the tomatoes in boiling water for a minute or so, until they are easy to peel. Peel, halve, and seed them; set aside in a bowl.

Separate the garlic cloves and peel them. Put them in an ovenproof baking dish in 1/4 cup of the olive oil and put them in the oven.

Meanwhile, heat up the rest of the olive oil in a cast-iron skillet and place the tomatoes, cut side down, in the hot oil to sear. When they start to darken (3 to 4 minutes), remove them to the baking dish with the garlic. Salt and pepper them and continue roasting until the garlic starts to turn golden and the tomatoes are sizzling — about 30 to 40 minutes. Check regularly to make sure they don't burn.

In the meantime, cook the spaghetti in the boiling water until it is very al dente (it will finish cooking in the hot oil), I would say 7 to 8 minutes, tops. When the tomatoes and garlic are perfect, add the drained pasta to the baking dish, toss, add the crushed red pepper, and place back in the oven for a couple of minutes, letting the pasta drink up the flavors of the vegetables. Sprinkle the basil on top and serve with Parmesan cheese.

Spaghetti in Parchment Paper

Serves 4

This recipe used to be called Spaghetti in Aluminum Foil until I found out that kitchen parchment is a lot sexier. If you can get it, the parchment does work a little better and is more pleasing to the eye. But if you can't find it, substitute foil rather than some other kind of paper that may have chemicals or an odd flavor that will ruin the dish. Like the recipe above, this uses some pretty basic ingredients, but it is radically enhanced by the unusual cooking method.

1 1/2 pounds ripe plum tomatoes	1 1/2 cups marinara sauce
1 pound spaghetti	parsley, chopped
1/2 pound black wrinkly olives, pitted	salt and freshly ground pepper
	Parmesan cheese

Preheat the oven to 375 degrees.

Blanch the tomatoes in boiling water for a minute or so, remove, and peel them as soon as you can touch them. Cut them in half, remove the seeds, and set them aside.

Cook the pasta for a bit less time than usual, about 7 or 8 minutes, because it will finish cooking in the parchment. When the pasta is ready, add it to the bowl with the tomatoes; add the pitted olives with a little of their oil, the marinara sauce, parsley, salt, and pepper and mix well.

Set out 4 pieces of parchment or foil and divide the mixture among them. Tightly close each package and put on a baking sheet in the oven for 15 minutes or so. Serve with cheese.

ॐ

This next recipe uses boneless, skinned turkey breast (often sold in stores as turkey cutlets). When we were skimping in the early days, turkey was a frequent substitute for veal scallopini.

There's very little loss in flavor and maybe an improvement in texture.

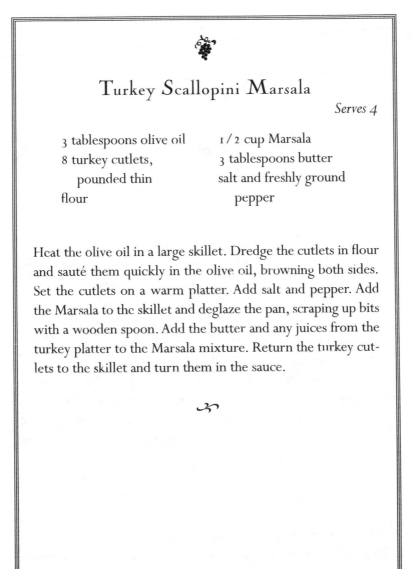

Turkey Scallopini Marsala

Serves 4

3 tablespoons olive oil	1/2 cup Marsala
8 turkey cutlets,	3 tablespoons butter
pounded thin	salt and freshly ground
flour	pepper

Heat the olive oil in a large skillet. Dredge the cutlets in flour and sauté them quickly in the olive oil, browning both sides. Set the cutlets on a warm platter. Add salt and pepper. Add the Marsala to the skillet and deglaze the pan, scraping up bits with a wooden spoon. Add the butter and any juices from the turkey platter to the Marsala mixture. Return the turkey cutlets to the skillet and turn them in the sauce.

Scraping Bottom

 The romantic image of two artists living in a ramshackle garret in Greenwich Village, starving for their muse, was great — for about a month. Then it was less than great; and it quickly became exactly what it was: tedious, anxiety-producing, and totally without air-conditioning. The weekly trips to the unemployment line were a sobering reminder of just how unromantic our idyll had become.

I was at a complete loss as to how to jump-start my career in New York. All my credits were from repertory theaters and were singularly unimpressive to New York agents and producers. Early on I had wrangled an appointment with a William Morris agent, who was the son of a friend of a cousin, or something like that. He sat behind his gleaming desk and handled my résumé as if it were a used Kleenex.

"I'd really have to see you in something," he said, his eyes shifting. I leaped to my feet and launched into a monologue — a stream-of-consciousness piece adapted from James Joyce's

Ulysses that I'm sure had never been heard before or since in the offices of William Morris. As I finished the speech, a Joycean jumble of disjointed images and phrases, my eyes filled with tears, my Irish accent still reverberating off the Plexiglas picture frames of celebrities that gleamed at me from the wall behind him, I became aware of an odd expression on his face. I had never seen anything quite like it — an undisguised sneer on his lips mixed with a gleam in his eye that said, "Wait till I tell the guys at lunch about *this* one."

Jill's career, however, showed occasional signs of life; a manager signed her for representation, and she began to go to auditions and meetings on a fairly regular basis. Then she landed a job in an off-Broadway production of *The Beggar's Opera* directed by an old friend of mine, who seemingly never even considered that *I* might need a job. She left for work six nights a week with a lightness in her step and a sparkle in her eyes that I envied, and then began to resent. She tried not to show her happiness — poor baby, she desperately tried not to enjoy herself in front of me, but she's never been able to hide anything. She's transparent — one of the reasons she's such a wonderful actress and one of the features that makes her so utterly beautiful.

She would leave for the show after an early dinner and I would sit at the window with Alison on my lap and look down on Perry Street from four floors up. We watched Jill walk to the corner, turn right, and disappear toward the Sheridan Square subway station. We waved until we could see her no more. It was August and the evenings were hot and airless and interminably long. I knew she wouldn't be back until after dark, and dark was a long time away.

I would never work again, I thought. New York was too big a

pond, too competitive; I wasn't the actor I once was, or even worse, I was never the actor I once thought I was. Jill's success framed my failure; her movement defined my stasis. She was performing every night on a stage under bright lights while people sat in the darkness and adored her. I was doing the dishes. In the *best* of times, I don't like doing dishes; when fifty million people watched me on TV and I was the toast of five continents, I didn't like doing dishes. So, you can imagine.

I helped Alison on with her shoes and we went out into the sultry streets for ice cream, and then to Abington Square to play on the swings or maybe to Washington Square to watch the street performers and the junkies. She was tiny but bright as a penny. She asked questions and I answered. That was my job. When all else failed, I was a father; I was needed and looked up to (she was very short at the time). I was unconditionally loved — and I answered most of the questions. It was a good job.

When we finished the ice cream and were done with the swings, we sat on a park bench like old men and watched the dusk fall.

"Sometimes I just like to sit here and watch people," I said. She looked at me very seriously and nodded, not comprehending why this might be fun.

"People are interesting," I added. She nodded again and we were silent for a moment.

"There's one," she said helpfully. I had a great assistant.

One day while combing through the trade papers for work, I came across an ad that said, "Be a live cartoon," and gave a number to call. Well, it wasn't Chekhov, but it was a hell of a lot better than "Nude male models — great pay!" so I checked it out.

It turned out to be a business that specialized in trade shows and sales meetings for large corporations. Their gimmick was a device that combined puppetry and videotronics into a cartoon that appeared live on a TV screen. The cartoon figure could see you and hear you and hold a conversation with you — all controlled by an unseen actor-puppeteer who was cleverly hidden from view. It was very effective, and as far as I know, the company is still successful today. I was to be a cartoon trainee.

I attacked this opportunity with a ferocity I didn't know existed in me. Every ounce of frustration and anger and desperation that I felt as a result of my rejection by the New York theater world fueled my assault on the live-cartoon industry. I was a smashing success. I was soon performing at such impressive venues as the Dallas Auto Show and the SmithKline and French Pharmaceuticals national sales meeting. Surely you caught my act.

In a very short time I graduated to writing the material, for that was where the money was. And I started making it hand over fist. I was a man possessed, writing two, sometimes three scripts at a time. I quickly paid my debts and opened a savings account. I never realized how important money was to me until I started making it. It was like an aphrodisiac, a potent symbol of achievement and recognition. And not only money, but power too. I met with executives from large, famous, stock-exchange-type corporations and, with input, wrote their speeches and formulated their sales meetings. I was peeking over the fence into the world of business and finance, the world of my father and brother, the world I had shunned all my life, and I found that I could succeed there. Captains of industry, silver-haired sharks with thousand-dollar suits and red power ties, actual grown-ups, turned to me for advice. Because I could teach them what four years at the Wharton School of Business could never teach them — to humanize themselves so that their audience would warm up to them, so that their message would go down easier; to loosen themselves up so they could give the impression of having a self-deprecating sense of humor; to appear like regular guys; to capture the empathy of their audience and hold it until their point was driven home. No wonder they paid me a lot.

I put my art on hold. I shoved my love for the theater into cold storage and closed the door tightly. I didn't want to think about it or hear about it. Jill's career progressed and that was fine — for her. But I was the breadwinner, the hunter-gatherer, the caveman that lurks just below the surface of every man. Whatever I had learned about acting and character development and the subtle art of manipulating an audience's emotions I turned to the sole purpose of making money.

We moved to the Upper West Side into a large, comfortable apartment; we bought furniture. We started collecting art. We put Alison into a private school. I had made it; I had finally achieved the middle-class success that I had spent all those years trying to avoid. What I didn't realize is that money is a much more complicated beast than it appears to be. You always have to pay — one way or the other. I couldn't see that I was getting paid in inverse proportion to the amount of satisfaction I felt. This formula has held true to this day; I think it's as immutable as the law of gravity: the more fun I have, the less money I get paid — and vice versa. For example, if I am asked to do a dandruff commercial where I have to stand nude in a shower with half my head covered with one shampoo and half my head with another, all to be shown daily on national television, I can get paid many thousands of dollars — for one day's work. But if I want to act in Chekhov's *Three Sisters* and have a rich, stimulating artistic experience, I'll be lucky to make a few hundred a week, and most likely I'll have to pay *them* for the privilege. It is the way of life. If they know you're having fun, why should they pay you for it? They're not having any fun; why should you?

One side effect of my venture into the world of business was that I stopped cooking. I had a colander full of excuses: I was too busy, my heart wasn't in it, I could afford to go out to restaurants, and so on. Whatever the excuses, we ended up eating out more often than not, or ordering take-out from one of the many great Szechuan or Shanghai restaurants on the Upper West Side. We were on a first-name basis with all the delivery boys. "Whatsa matter, Mr. Tucker? No dumplings tonight?"

Then at Christmas, in an act of infinite wisdom and subtlety, Jill saved my soul — once again — from eternal shallowness. She gave me a gift of cooking lessons at the China Institute to study under the eminent teacher and cookbook author, Florence Lin. I guess she figured if we were eating Chinese every night anyway, at least we could get some that was home cooked. But of course there was more to it than that; what she was really doing was a bit of deglazing. My creative juices had dried up and gotten stuck to the bottom of the pan, so to speak. The only thing I was creating was money, and that wasn't enough to sustain me. My energies were shrinking, my vision was narrowing, and my wardrobe was getting altogether too J. Press. Jill's gift was a gentle shove, reminding me of my need to create — it was a glass of potent wine that loosened all the stuck-on, dried-up bits of my soul and bubbled them back to life. Have I taken that metaphor far enough?

Mrs. Lin's class was a hoot — eleven housewives from Long

Island and me. My classmates distrusted me at first. They treated me like some infidel who had come to steal the secrets of their coven. But I soon emerged as the teacher's pet. Mrs. Lin loved my enthusiasm and my knack for cooking and just generally thought I was adorable — and that forced my class-mates to look at me in a different light. Soon they accepted my presence in their all-female enclave and started treating me like a scruffy little pet. I was kind of the golden retriever of Mrs. Lin's Monday, Wednesday, Friday class.

We toured Chinatown, learned about ingredients, haggled with the merchants, and bought utensils and bottled sauces. We had Chinese history and culture lectures and also got a glimpse into Mrs. Lin's personal odyssey from mainland China to the East Side of Manhattan. But most of all we cooked.

For me it was a totally new way of looking at the art of cooking. It was so organized! Chop and slice and mince and measure, then put everything in little bowls before you even think of turning on the flame. I had always cooked instinc-tively, and at first I resisted what appeared to be a dogmatic insistence on exactness and neatness and a military regulation of size and shape. But when I tasted my first dish, I was de-lighted — it actually tasted like Chinese food! It was as if I had performed a card trick to the amazement of my family and friends. "My God, Michael, this tastes like the stuff we get at Chun Cha Fu!" If I had put it into those little cardboard car-tons, they would never have known the difference. And the theatrical possibilities were a big draw too. Cooking Chinese all happens in a matter of seconds over a very hot flame — after tedious hours of preparing everything that goes into those little bowls — and the resulting moment of creation is not unlike a fireworks display, complete with fire, smoke, and noise. And it's really not at all difficult.

Stir-Fried Pork with Broccoli

Serves 4

This was my first dish with Mrs. Lin, and I've put it together from memory. It's simple and quick and should be served with rice.

2 tablespoons corn-
starch
2 tablespoons soy sauce
1 tablespoon sherry
1 / 2 pound lean pork,
sliced into thin strips
about 1 / 2 inch wide
and 1 1 / 2 inches
long (partially
freeze the pork;
it's easier to slice
thin)

2 tablespoons peanut
oil
1 head broccoli sepa-
rated into florets,
stalks peeled and
sliced into 1-inch
lengths
1 / 2 cup chicken broth

Mix together 1 tablespoon of the cornstarch, 1 tablespoon of the soy sauce, and the sherry. Add the pork and marinate for a half hour or so.

Heat the oil in a wok, swirling it around so it covers most of the surface; when it is very hot but not smoking, add the marinated pork strips. Stir-fry until the pork loses all its pink color, then remove to a plate.

Add a little more oil, if necessary. Heat to very hot, then add the broccoli. Stir-fry for 2 minutes or so.

Add the chicken broth and create a little well in the center of the wok where the liquid gathers, leaving the broccoli all around it. Cover and let steam for 3 to 4 minutes.

Meanwhile, mix together the remaining 1 tablespoon of cornstarch and 1 tablespoon of soy sauce with 1 tablespoon of water. Uncover the wok and add the soy sauce mixture to the liquid. Stir and let thicken. Return the pork to the wok, stir to heat thoroughly, and serve.

Steamed Whole Fish

Serves 6

This is a wonderful banquet kind of dish to have as the climax of a Chinese meal. It is as delicate as the stir-fry is dramatic; the scallions, ginger, and soy sauce add just enough flavor to enhance the delicacy of the fish. It's also simple to do, and you can use your wok as an improvised steamer. The most important aspect of this dish is the shopping. If you come up with a perfectly fresh fish, this can be a transcendent dish, so you must approach your local fish merchant with a keen eye, a sensitive touch, and an all-knowing nose. Look your fish in the eye; make sure it's clear and bright. Touch its flesh; make sure it's firm. Ask the merchant if it's absolutely fresh. If you ask him real fast, he may be surprised enough to tell you the truth. If it's not fresh, cook something else today and wait until you can find the perfect fish.

1 (1 1/2-pound) whole fish, preferably sea bass, cleaned and gutted but with the head and tail on	1 tablespoon sesame oil
	1/2 teaspoon sugar
	coarse salt
	2 tablespoons ginger, thinly shredded
1 tablespoon soy sauce	peanut oil
1 tablespoon sherry	1 scallion, shredded

Wash the fish inside and out and pat dry. Then score it crosswise with a sharp knife at 1-inch intervals all along its length on both sides.

Combine the soy sauce, sherry, sesame oil, and sugar.

Rub the salt over the fish, inside and out. Then place it on a heatproof dish that will fit inside your wok. Pour the soy sauce mixture over the fish, then arrange the ginger shreds over that.

Fashion your steamer by placing a small bowl half-filled with water in the bottom of your wok. The water will stabilize the bowl. Then put 2 cups or so of water around the bowl in the wok itself. Turn the heat on until the water boils. Then place the plate with the fish on the stabilized bowl, cover the wok tightly, and steam for 12 to 14 minutes. Don't peek.

When the fish is about done, heat a few tablespoons of peanut oil in a small sauté pan almost to smoking. Check the fish for doneness: if it's springy to the touch, it's done. When just ready, scatter the scallions over the fish and carefully spatter the hot oil over the scallions.

NINE

Monday Nights

🍇

⤷ Everything was dropping nicely into place. Money was coming in on a regular basis, Jill's career was gaining momentum, I was cooking again, and the final papers for my divorce came through. We decided to celebrate all this by getting married. It seemed a good idea for a number of reasons. Alison was three years old and had been living with us since the separation. Although the divorce granted me official custody, Jill's position was undefined even though she had taken on all the responsibilities of motherhood. We decided our getting legal would solidify the situation for all concerned. Also, we loved each other; also, we wanted the presents. And Alison made a picture-perfect flower girl. We sent out invitations that read "Alison Tucker cordially invites you to the wedding of her parents." Both families were properly shocked.

Despite our posthippie lifestyle and back-street beginnings, it turned out to be a typical middle-class wedding after all, filled with people who wouldn't have given each other the time of day were they not somehow related — either by blood or by the ceremony they were brought together to witness. Jill's mom and dad hadn't laid eyes on each other since they split some ten years before. Their public reunion set the tone for the event — strained conviviality and forced heartiness. It was, as I said, a pretty typical wedding. My parents, who thought their son totally devoid of any sense of responsibility, viewed this second marriage with the same grim optimism Columbus's parents must have felt as they waved good-bye from the dock, knowing he would shortly sail off the edge of the earth. Little did they know I was about to discover the New World.

Rabbi Joseph Gelberman was chosen to officiate. We hoped he would please all parents; mine for obvious reasons, and Jill's because his tenure at the Hunter College philosophy department would satisfy their Unitarian needs. He was also the only rabbi we could find who would marry us without Jill's converting to Judaism. Joe Gelberman turned out to be quite a find. The fact that we found him through the Yellow Pages is one of the strongest arguments I know of for predestination. He invited us down to the Little Synagogue in the Village to partake in a service. When we heard the wisdom and tolerance and soaring humanity of his sermon, we knew we had our man. He also looked the part. Central casting couldn't have come up with a wiser, kinder, fuzzier-looking rabbi.

The festivities were separated into two parts: a wedding ceremony for family and close friends in the early afternoon, and a blowout party for the multitudes that night, both taking place in our apartment. This was a huge mistake. Nobody went home in between. All the out-of-town relatives just stayed. "Would you like a little more cake, Uncle Lee?" I asked blearily at five-thirty in the afternoon. Jill and Alison and I finally fled the apartment, leaving relatives from both sides to stare at each other for a bit while we rented a hansom cab at the Plaza and rode it through the park all the way home to Eighty-ninth Street.

I don't remember much else, except for the food. Thank God for the food. We catered the ceremony from Murray's Sturgeon Shop, which was right up the street on Broadway. In its heyday there was no better smoked fish in all of New York. Murray's countermen sliced smoked salmon like brain surgeons doing the most intricate lobotomy. Our wedding platter was festooned with slices of lox, nova, and sturgeon, which cost a king's ransom, and the lowly, bargain-basement sable, which was my favorite. Why was it my favorite? Because it had more fat, of course. Sable just seemed to slide itself into the scallion cream cheese, which in turn melted into the fresh, still-hot bagel. It made for a fairly perfect bite. The crowning touch was a giant bowl filled with Murray's herring, which was proudly made on the premises. There were a number of different styles, but my favorite was and is the pickled herring in cream sauce with onions — a triumph of texture and taste, with the voluptuously tender fillets of briny herring mixed with the sweetness of the cream sauce and the occasional sweet-strong crunch of thin-sliced raw onion. It was worth the gallons of water you had to drink over the next few days to compensate for the salt intake.

These platters, plus baskets of bagels, bialys, and challah got us through the afternoon. And of course there was the wedding cake. Specially constructed by Miss Grimbel of Columbus Avenue, it was a two-layer cheesecake with the appropriate congratulations written on top in colors to match the bride's dress. With the photographers poised, Jill and I held the cake knife together in the traditional manner and started to make the first cut. The knife wouldn't go through. We pushed harder. Still, no luck. Was the cake frozen solid? Were we so exhausted from making a life commitment that we couldn't push a knife through eight pounds of soft Philadelphia cream cheese? Friends leaped to our aid; more, sharper, knives were sought, but no one could hack through this cake. Was this an omen? Was this a symbol? No, Miss Grimbel had inserted a steel plate between the layers so they wouldn't ooze into each other and had neglected to mention it to anybody. We have pictures of this debacle taken from every unphotogenic angle possible.

Thus ended the more formal part of the day. But the party that night was a different animal. It was for our friends, who were, for the most part, struggling actors, writers, and directors who wanted to raise the roof a bit in celebration of our marriage. It was a bring-your-own-booze kind of event. And for the food we decided on something a little different, something casual and very New York.

Gus the hot dog man was a fixture on the corner of Eighty-ninth and Riverside in front of the Soldiers and Sailors Memorial at the entrance to Riverside Park. We knew Gus quite well because it was genetically impossible for me to pass his cart without having a hot dog with sauerkraut, mustard, and those "New York" onions in spicy red sauce that only hot dog men have the recipe for. We asked Gus if he could haul his cart up to our apartment and serve hot dogs all night to our friends, and he thought this was a great idea. There was a touchy moment when our landlord caught Gus firing up the propane in the service elevator, but finally we managed to get him all set up, with the blue-and-yellow Sabrett's umbrella taking up a good part of the dining room and a line of happy eaters stretching out down the hallway and into the living room. Gus rose to the occasion. He doled out not only a record number of hot dogs but also a little piece of Greek wisdom to each customer.

Jill's midwestern brood, my Baltimore relatives, and the mad crush of sixties-generated substance abusers that made up our friends were all doing their best to bridge the generation gap over the music coming out of the pumped-up stereo. The party kicked into high gear. My friend Marc Flanagan, hot dog and drink in hand, spotted an obvious relative — an aunt, almost certainly — sitting alone in the corner of the living room and decided to make her feel part of the party.

"You must be Michael's aunt," he said, shaking her hand. This was a good guess; she was dark and European looking and clearly not one of Jill's Nordic-looking brood.

"I'm sorry?" she said in a thick accent.

"Michael's aunt," Marc said louder.

"Michael?" replied the lady, clearly confused.

"The groom. Michael, the groom." There was a long silence as they looked at each other, perplexed.

"I am the wife of the hot dog man," she said proudly.

A few weeks after the wedding, just as I thought I had achieved some sort of stability in my life, I got a call from Zelda Fitchandler. She was the founder and artistic director of Arena Stage in Washington, D.C., where Jill and I had met and courted. She wanted to know if I was interested in playing a small part in a production of Brecht's *The Resistible Rise of Arturo Ui,* to start in Washington in a couple of weeks. Well, this was the last thing I needed. I had given up acting; it had beaten, frustrated, and humiliated me. Besides, I was happily embarked on a profitable career in the sales-meeting business, which demanded all my time and attention. If I left to go play actor for ten weeks, you could be damn sure the job wouldn't be waiting for me when I got back. Also, I didn't want to be separated from Jill and Alison for ten weeks. No way. It was out of the question. I couldn't afford it — not financially, and certainly not emotionally. And the part wasn't any good. If I was going to give up all this money and security and ego gratification, at the very least I should be playing the leading role! Zelda calmly reasserted that the job was mine if I wanted it and to let her know as soon as possible. Now, I don't know to this day whether she knew that I had left the business and was tempting me back, or whether she was just short one short actor and I filled the bill. But either way, I guess I owe her a thank-you.

Yes, that's right; I took the job. The call of the ham bone was too strongly entrenched in my soul to ignore. The sad fact is that I've never been able to turn down an acting job. Big or small, comical or tragical, cinematical or theatrical, I tend to take the job. I'm an acting whore. Always was, always will be.

Thus began one of the more interesting periods of my life. I worked Tuesdays through Sundays down in Washington and spent Mondays back at home in New York. Once the show opened, I found myself out of town with no responsibilities during the day and I hoped to spend that time writing my sales-meeting scripts. I told the company I could do input meetings on Mondays when I was in New York, and by phone when I wasn't, and send the finished scripts back to them by mail. I tried like hell to convince them this would work, because I really didn't want to see that money go into somebody else's pocket, but, as usual, art and commerce were not comfortable in bed together. They decided I didn't love them anymore and replaced me without so much as a second thought. So, I was a poor artist again. By default, I grant you, but an artist again nonetheless.

Meanwhile, back in New York, Mondays were complicated. Besides cramming a week's worth of head-of-household chores into one day, I felt I needed to spend time with Alison to remind her that she had a father who was not just some little guy who crept in and slept with her mother once a week. That took care of the mornings and the afternoons. And Monday nights were for Jill and me to catch up, to make the necessary repairs that we always need after even the smallest separation, to put patches on the small leaks that seem to crop up in the intimacy and trust departments. The problem was that Jill had an acting class on Monday nights. My first reaction was to take it personally. After all, this was our only night together. Was this a way of showing me she didn't need me? But then I realized Jill doesn't work that way. She was zoned in on this class. She has a way of focusing on important tasks and not easing up until she masters them. She's a bulldog. And this class was crucial to her as an actor. It was going to take her to the next step, the next plateau in her development as an artist. All I wanted to do was have dinner. We compromised. She would take her class, which went until nine, and then we would have a late dinner at Alfredo's after. I — not to be outdone in the artistic department — enrolled in a playwriting class at the New School that met at roughly the same time as her acting class.

So every Monday night we went off to our respective classes, met afterward, and walked through the streets of the West Village to Bank and Hudson Streets, the home of the Trattoria Da Alfredo. We babbled about what we had learned that night, about the trade secrets that had been revealed to us, about the energies we felt had been released in us. I remember walking through the rain one night and not feeling a drop. We were so engrossed in ourselves and each other that we were impervious to the elements, the traffic, the muggers; we walked under the protective umbrella of artistic smugness, boundless ardor, and the youthful assurance that all the excitement lay before us and we would never die. By the time we got to Alfredo's, we were famished.

Alfredo's had been our discovery. We were regulars long before it became a hot ticket. We knew Alfredo Viazzi; we knew his wife (the wonderful actress Jane White); we knew what to order; we knew what wine to buy at the liquor store up the street because Alfredo had no liquor license. We knew, because we were old and valued customers, that he would offer us a glass of anisette from his private stock to savor after dinner. We watched the other diners wonder who we were to get such preferential treatment.

We ate too much. Jill was not quite as extravagant as I, of course, but even she managed four courses. We couldn't pass up sampling everything the kitchen had to offer. Fortunately, this was 1973 and cholesterol hadn't yet been invented.

We had baked clams first. Fresh littlenecks stuffed with garlic, bread crumbs, Parmesan cheese, fresh herbs (oregano, thyme, basil, and parsley), all mixed together in a little sherry, clam juice, and olive oil. Each clam was covered with a spoonful of the stuffing, baked for fifteen minutes, and then finished under the broiler so that the top came out all sizzly-crusty. We squeezed lemon over the tops.

Then came an order of the stuffed mushrooms. These too were first baked, then finished under the broiler. The stuffing was a mixture of prosciutto, Genoa salami, ham, herbs, and Parmesan cheese. Alfredo put them first into the oven in a baking dish with a little chicken stock, then sizzled them under the broiler. We ate both these dishes with crusty bread to soak up the juices on our plates.

Then we had a little salad "to cleanse the palate." This is one of the greatest lies in all of gastronomy. There was more fat in those salads than in a large pepperoni pizza, but because we said the magic *salad* word, we convinced ourselves we were eating bunny food. One of our favorites was a spinach salad with mushrooms, topped with a rich vinaigrette, and then finished with a thick piece of bacon cut in chunks and cooked in butter. Oh, Alfredo!

The pasta course was spaghetti carbonara, a light little dish with the noodles nestled in bacon, egg, cheese, and cream. Or green tagliarini ai quatro formaggi — with butter, cream, and four cheeses. Jill loved that one, being a Wisconsin girl who had grown up on macaroni and cheese. Or paglia e fieno, which means "hay and straw" — green and yellow strands of fresh fettucine in one of the most soul-satisfying sauces I've ever tasted: sweet sausage, mushrooms, garlic, herbs, cream, and butter. Or tortellini with prosciutto and peas in — what else? — butter and cheese.

Then we'd move on to the main dishes — fish for Jill, veal for me. And always with perfectly cooked green beans on the side. The secret of the beans is to parboil them in salty water for two to three minutes, then drain them and immediately cover them with ice-cold water or even ice cubes. Finally, toss them in a hot sauté pan in butter. Simple and great. Sometimes we'd share a huge pot of cacciucco alla Livornese, a pungent, tomatoey fish soup, redolent with garlic, onion, herbs, and hot pepper that penetrated the fish fillets and shrimps with a powerful hot-sweet flavor. There was plenty of crusty bread to dip in the broth, of course.

I don't remember ever eating dessert. Sorry. But with a bottle each of white wine and red wine plus anisette after, we had all the sugar our systems could handle. We embraced Alfredo and staggered out onto Hudson Street and wandered through the Village in a happy stupor. We had fed our souls, then our bellies; then we hailed a cab to go home and feed our love.

One Monday night we were lying in bed, the room illuminated by a bright street lamp that stood right outside our window. We were quiet for a long time, thinking about the evening, the classes, the dinner; thinking about each other and that I was going away again in the morning.

"Do you like acting again?" asked Jill. "How does it feel?"

"Good. It feels like I'm good at it. It feels like it's what I should be doing."

We let that sink in for a while.

"I don't know why I have trouble up here," I said finally. "It's like New York freezes me."

I watched Jill's eyes in the light of the street lamp. She was thinking hard. It suddenly occurred to me that she was going to tell me why. My muscles tensed as if I were about to be hit. She said nothing for a long time. Then she turned to me and stroked my face with her finger.

"You don't let yourself show when you act," she said. "This warm, vulnerable, funny person that I love so much, and that our friends love, doesn't show. You don't let him out."

A cold finger moved up my spine. It's hard for me to take advice, or even worse, criticism — especially about acting — especially from Jill. I was competitive with her. I felt I needed to hold the power in the relationship or she wouldn't need me — wouldn't love me. And deep down, I felt I was the better actor; I don't think that anymore, but in those days it seemed important.

The odd thing was I didn't get angry. She was so brave to say it; she certainly knew the risks. I was so blown away by her courage, I forgot to get defensive. And anger wasn't what I felt, anyway. I felt a bit confused, and sad for all the time lost. I had learned in school that to be a character actor, I had to "disappear" into the roles, so that none of me could be seen — and I had always admired actors who could do that. But, in doing so, I had buried the prism that all the light has to shine through if any real expression is going to take place. How could I have missed that?

I started to cry. Not out of sadness, out of love. And Jill cried too. And an incredible thought shot through me: "I'm lying here naked with another person. It's not a man-woman thing, just two human beings." It was a startling thought; we were two naked people trying to figure it all out — not really succeeding; maybe you never do — but realizing we trusted each other enough to try to do it together.

TEN

The Bearded Clam

❧

‿❧ I wish I could say that everything fell easily into place after my return to the acting profession, but this is not a work of fiction. I went back to the hard pavements of New York and auditioned for work. I kept banging my head against the casting-office doors, and occasionally they opened a crack. But there was a difference; I felt a new confidence in myself. Maybe this was because I had lived in New York for a couple of years and was less intimidated; maybe my success in the corporate world gave me the boost I needed, or maybe I was just flat-out tired of rejection. Whatever it was, I was finding it easier not to take no for an answer. Is that clear?

Mostly my confidence came from the fact that I had found the secret, the time-tested, foolproof method of finding a job in the theater: make other plans — that's all there is to it. Commit time and money and expectation to a vacation or a summer house in the country, and without fail, a job will come along to prevent you from enjoying it.

Well, I had made such a plan just before going off to Washington. My old buddy Bruce came up with the idea of renting a beach house in Fairfield, Connecticut. We convinced Marc and Mary Flanagan to join in so that among us we could manage the three-month rental fee. In the years to come, Don Scardino and Lizzie Lathram joined in as well. Then Mary Beth Hurt, Victor Garber, Jim Jansen, and others. But the core group always stayed the same.

I got back from Washington in May and was all set to take the summer off and spend time with my family and friends at the beach. "Aha!" said the gods. "Are you all set? Have you made the deposit? Has the check cleared? Good! Here's a job. Break a leg!" And this was to be the pattern for the next four or five years: we'd commit to the beach house, and two weeks later we'd both get work that took us away for at least part of the summer. But in truth it was great; we had nothing to complain about. We shuttled back and forth between work and play, between dedication and hedonism (which I was also dedicated to), and I look back on it as one of the best times of my life. Thank God we were young.

An actor I met in Washington was going right into a production of *Merry Wives of Windsor* at Joe Papp's Shakespeare in the Park. He was a friend of the director's and managed to get me an audition without my having to go through the usual channels of agent, casting director, producer, director. I read, got called back to read for Joe Papp, and got the part. This was more like it! The Public Theater was a perfect place for me, a natural transition from my repertory background to the New York stage. It seemed that if I could avoid agents and casting directors, I'd be able to find work easily; this paradox has been true for me throughout my career.

I played a character named Simple, and although it wasn't a

large part, Simple and I got along just fine. He was the first in a long line of Shakespearean parts I was to play of characters with dumb, self-descriptive names — Simple, Froth, Flute, Scum, Slurp — I've played them all.

Oh, I had a good time in the Park; it was summer acting camp. The actors and the audience seemed to be suspended in a state of grace there. I think it was because we all felt we were there for a higher purpose — other than merely having a good time. And that, of course, allowed us to *really* have a good time. We were celebrating the fact that we had survived another day in New York. We were reaffirming that Our Town was more than the filthy, sweltering, crime-infested, eardrum shattering hellhole that we staggered around in all day. At night it was transformed into a vernal, moonlit park where we could take a picnic and watch and perform some pretty fair poetry every evening — all for free. We felt civilized and terribly evolved.

Merry Wives is an earthy, sexy romp that portrays the rural, marital dilemmas of the Fords (Marcia Rodd and Joe Bova) and the Pages (Cynthia Harris and George Hearn), along with the meddling of Mistress Quickly and the indefatigable John Falstaff, played by Marilyn Sokol and the indefatigable Barnard Hughes (Barney was to go on to play Jill's father the following fall in a play that was to have a long run on Broadway, so he became a member of the family, so to speak). I was in good company. I was acting. I was earning a living. Now, if I could only get up to the beach house, life would be perfect. During rehearsals I sneaked up there on my Mondays off, but once we opened — in mid-June — I was determined to make the hour train commute on a daily basis.

The last train for Connecticut left Grand Central Station at 11:00 P.M., and there was no way I could get there in time. But it made a stop in Harlem at 125th Street at around 11:20, and if the show started on time and we didn't milk the laughs too much and the taxi ran all the lights, I could just get there in time to catch it. So every night, right after the final company bow, the audience would file out of the park — only to see Simple, in his street clothes, bounding past them to steal the first taxi coming up Central Park West.

"In faith, a merry night unto you all," I would shout out the taxi window in pure Shakespearean iambic pentameter as I sped on my way to Harlem.

We named our house the Bearded Clam, an appropriately nautical allusion. We all pitched in and bought a car for $150 — a twelve-year-old Ford Country Squire that was immediately renamed the Village Idiot. We tended to name things in those days. The little second-hand dinghy that we picked up was known as the *Edna Mae Breakwind,* and a fine sailing vessel she was.

We indulged ourselves at the beach in every way known to man with substances legal and illegal. This was the seventies, we were young and immortal and on vacation. There was no holding us back. Now, let it be known that during the run of the show, I held my substance abuse down to a dull roar, but come mid-July I was a free man and was able to indulge my appetites unchecked.

One afternoon in August, I was taking a break from the sun, sitting in an overstuffed chair in the living room, propping a good book on my overstuffed tummy, trying to focus through a pungent haze of marijuana, when a cry of alarm came up from the beach. Stoned as I was, I managed to get up from the chair to go see what was happening. Marc Flanagan was sitting in the sand with an anxious group around him, and I could see when I got there that he was bleeding pretty badly. He had stepped on the appropriately named razor clam and gashed the bottom of his foot. There was some discussion of getting the first-aid kit until we all concluded that we didn't own a first-aid kit. I ran to get a quart of vodka, which we splashed over the cut. Fortunately, we had an ample supply of that.

"We need bandages and iodine," said Mary — ever the attentive mother in an emergency.

"I'll go," I volunteered, and ran into the house to put my sandals on.

I leaped into the Village Idiot, which was a huge old boat of a station wagon; I could barely see over the steering wheel. Its engine started only one out of five tries, so it didn't really qualify as an emergency vehicle, but amazingly, that day it sputtered right into life and I was on my way to save the day.

By the time I pulled into the parking lot of the A&P, my cannabis-smoked brain had completely forgotten its mission.

"No problem," I thought. "It'll come to me."

I charged into the air-conditioned, neon-lit world of the supermarket with high hopes, grabbed a shopping cart, and headed down one of the aisles. Somehow I remembered that I was in a hurry, but I'll be damned if I could come up with a reason for it.

I picked up a six-pack of diet soda. We always needed that. Chips? No, too fattening — got to cut down on the old carbos, I thought. And then I came face to face with my old nemesis — salted in the shell peanuts.

"I'll get two bags," I thought. "May as well stock up." And then, suddenly, my conscience blinked its eyes and half woke up.

"I have to get something for someone other than myself," it said.

This was a foreign thought and I stood there for a while trying to adjust to it. What could I get that someone else needs? I thought long and hard. Finally I picked up a third bag of salted in the shell peanuts. This one would be for everyone else; I wouldn't even touch it. I felt suddenly purified — the way Mother Teresa must feel after one of her selfless deeds. I headed back to the beach with a light heart.

I pulled the car into the parking area behind the house and saw everyone standing there; it was as if they were waiting for me. I got out of the car and picked up the shopping bag filled with the peanuts and the diet soda and they all rushed down and took the bag from me. I had an uneasy feeling that for some reason they were taking away my peanuts.

"Hey," I articulated.

"Where are the bandages?" said Mary, looking frantically through the bag.

"Huh?" said I.

"Where's the iodine?"

I decided to hold my tongue. The circumstances were slowly coming back into focus and I didn't want to say anything that could be used against me later on.

Fortunately, Marc recovered and was able to walk again and the incident passed down into beach house lore. The fact that any of us survived this era with any of our brain cells intact is a miracle.

We had a parade of guests at the beach. Friends of every stripe leaped at the chance to escape the heat and oppression of New York, so we took turns inviting people up. It was a great way to get to know the other people's circle of friends and ultimately enlarge our own. I was often accused of being less than discriminating with my invitations. Anyone who came backstage after the show was invited up — if he was a friend, of course. Or an acquaintance. Or someone whom I always wanted to know. Or a friend of someone I'd always wanted to know. This became known as the Row K Syndrome, because my housemates accused me of walking out onto the stage every night at curtain call and inviting everyone sitting in row K to come up to Connecticut. In reality, it wasn't quite that bad.

Our guests always brought something that added to the beach house experience. One would be a sailing enthusiast and would teach us how to actually use our little boat for something more than a place to sit the kids when we had no more room at the table. One would bring a guitar and fill the evening with group songfests — John Lithgow regaled us many a time with his rendition of "Mr. McCloud Likes to Sing Real Loud," an original children's song that seemed to fit the beach house mentality to a T. Another would be into flower arranging and would make the house look like Martha Stewart's; another would be a photographer who documented the revels of the summer. Sometimes they would be young and attractive and would run around in skimpy bathing suits and kick up the libido level for the regulars. These were good guests.

And, of course, there were the bad guests. The occasional duds. We devised an award to be presented to the worst of these. It was called the Heinie and was awarded annually to the most heinous guests of the summer. There was some stiff competition. There was a couple who shall have to remain nameless who came with their children and their dog. The dog was a member of their family, they said proudly — and so, of course, he would have to be a member of ours as well. The dog bounded out of their car, ran to the beach, and crapped in front of Bruce's favorite deck chair — the one he slept in a good part of every day. How can I explain this? The fact that this dog did his business indiscriminately on our heretofore pristine beach just kind of ruined our summer. Suddenly we had land mines where none existed before. Every step we took had the potential of unpleasantness, to say the least. And our guests thought it was just great.

"Look how Kong loves the beach!" they beamed with pride. "We've got to get him out of the city more often."

They argued constantly with each other. Not openly, like Jewish people, but with little snipes and cuts, always in front of everyone. And when the tension mounted to the point of pain, the wife suddenly announced that she was going for a swim. She entered the water and swam out — straight out — for what seemed like miles, until we were sure that she was committing suicide. Her children stood on the shore, weeping, trying to find the speck that was their mother on the horizon. The dog howled. The husband smiled serenely, inwardly counting the insurance money. Mary called the Coast Guard. Finally Marc, who had learned to sail, took the *Edna Mae* out to find her. He had to lash her to the boat and haul her back in — just like in *The Old Man and the Sea*.

And they ate everything and brought nothing, of course. Their children were like Hoovers, sucking up food we didn't even know we had. We kept making trips to the A&P to replenish our supply, only to have it lapped up by these voracious, ungrateful little bastards. When the great moment came and they were actually departing — a day later than expected — we all stood on the back porch to watch their car disappear forever, when suddenly it stopped, backed up, and the youngest child jumped out, ran into the kitchen, and grabbed the last slice of bread in the house. And then, without a word, she jumped back into the car and they drove away.

Cooking took up a large part of the day at the beach. If we weren't actually doing it, we were talking about it or planning it. There were three categories: the cooks, the helpers, and the appreciators. Mary Flanagan and I were the cooks — always. Jill and Ceci were the helpers, and Marc and Bruce, the appreciators, whose job it was to grunt and squeal like little piggies with overenthusiastic delight at everything that was put in front of them. They were highly skilled professionals. They knew if their enthusiasm was lavish and vocal, no one would ask them to do any work. But if they slacked off — even for a second — if their *mmmmm*'s were a little perfunctory, their tummies not patted with the proper circular motion, they would quickly be up to their elbows in dishwater. They never faltered.

The helpers were essentially unskilled labor. I know I'm saying this about my own wife and it puts me in a delicate position, but setting the table and drying lettuce are not endeavors that require great skill or training. I know that Jill would take exception as regards the lettuce drying. She took — and still takes — her lettuce drying very seriously. She read somewhere that every drop of water that remains on the leaf dilutes the vinaigrette by that same amount. Now, she takes great pride in her salad dressing; it is her one and only culinary achievement. And the thought of common tap water invading the integrity of the delicate balance of oil, vinegar, and herbs so lovingly blended is anathema to her. So every piece of lettuce is first spun, then rolled in paper toweling, then individually inspected and daubed, first with a paper towel, then I think with a Q-tip to get those hard-to-reach little veiny sections of the romaine. Although it is this same devotion to detail that makes her such a wonderful actress — not to mention wife, mother, lover, and friend — I cannot in my heart consider lettuce drying an art form. Sorry, my darling.

Some days at low tide we would send Alison and Tara Flanagan, who were about five at the time, to dig for clams. Low tide was an exceptionally beautiful time, especially when it came toward evening and the sun was orange and low in the sky. The water of Long Island Sound receded hundreds of yards, creating a vast, flat, moistly packed playground in front of our house — for gulls to hunt for their dinner; for men to play Frisbee football, making impossible, heroic, diving catches and then splashing harmlessly into the soft arms of the Sound; for lovers to walk, ankle-deep in the warm, sudsy breakers, for miles, down to the end of the strand and back; and for daughters to dig for clams under the tutelage of Uncle Brucie, who grew up in the area and was wise to the ways of the Long Island soft-shell clams — otherwise known as steamers — also referred to by the children as pisser clams for their habit of squirting up a little stream of water when you stood on their hiding place in the wet sand, giving themselves away.

We washed and scrubbed them under cold water — dozens and dozens of them — then put them into a large pail, covered them with water, and sprinkled flour in. The theory was that they would eat the flour and then disgorge it, cleaning themselves in the process. I liked the idea of feeding the clams; it seemed the least we could do for them. Sometimes I would give them Italian food, adding a little oregano to the flour; sometimes a bit of cilantro for a Mexican treat.

These clam dinners worked best in August when the local corn and tomatoes were at their peak. White corn with the smallest kernels, the kind my dad used to call shoepeg corn, was the sweetest — when we could find it. It showed up at roadside stands, picked and sold by local farmers or by kids whose parents grew it in their backyards. Sometimes we boiled it or steamed it; sometimes we roasted it on the fire. But the only secret to great corn is to get great corn, fresh as tomorrow — and not to overcook it.

The best tomatoes were New Jersey tomatoes. Now, we were in Connecticut, where they grew fine tomatoes, and New York State was close by, but the best tomatoes were New Jersey tomatoes. Don't ask me why. The same was true when I grew up in Maryland. I remember waiting all year for the short, intense season, passing up the hard, plastic, supermarket tomatoes and the ones that said they came from some hothouse somewhere; they didn't make it either — any more than the tasteless beauties they serve up in California. But come late July or early August, suddenly the real tomatoes were everywhere. We all ate too many; we got little sores inside our mouths from the acid. But damn, they were good.

The evening always started with happy hour. Someone would say something about the sun being over the yardarm, and Bruce or I would stir up a pitcher of whatever drink was fashionable that summer. Sometimes margaritas, sometimes Silver Bullets, which were vodka martinis with a couple of cocktail onions. In later years we created the Naughty Mormon for Jimmy Jansen, which was a fiery blend of cassis and club soda. And Mary would start up the quesadillas, which were always part of what made happy hour happy. They were just flour tortillas scorched in a pan, filled with a combination of Jack and Cheddar cheeses and topped with sliced jalapeños and homemade salsa made with tomatoes, onions, and cilantro. We'd munch and sip, watch the sun go down, and think about the clams in their big old bucket.

Steamed Clams

To cook the clams, put just a half-cup of water in the bottom of a large pot. Bring it to a boil, then add the clams. Cover the pot and lower the heat to a simmer. Shake the pot to make sure all the clams cook evenly. You'll know they're done when the shells are all opened. If any refuse to open, throw them away.

Strain the broth in the bottom of the pot through some cheesecloth and put some in a bowl in front of each person. Melt some butter and do the same with that. Then divide up the clams into soup bowls and dive in. Remove the clam from its shell, remove the rubbery little foreskin from the end, swish the clam around in the broth to remove all grit, dip it into the butter, and pop it into your mouth.

Dessert was usually a plate of Killer Bea's. Mary's mom's name is Bea and she makes killer chocolate chip cookies. Here is the heretofore secret gem of a recipe.

Killer Bea's

Makes 3 dozen

2 1/4 cups triple-sifted
    flour (measure after
    sifting)
1 teaspoon salt
1 teaspoon baking soda
1 cup softened butter
1 cup firmly packed
    dark brown sugar

1 teaspoon vanilla
1/2 teaspoon water
1 egg
1 cup finely chopped
    walnuts
3 cups (1 1/2 pack-
    ages) chocolate bits

Preheat the oven to 375 degrees.

Sift together the dry ingredients; set aside. Combine the butter, sugar, vanilla, and water. Add the egg and beat until creamy. Add the dry ingredients; mix well. Stir in the walnuts and chocolate bits.

Line a cookie sheet with aluminum foil, shiny side up. Drop the cookie dough onto ungreased foil by the table-spoonful, about 1 inch apart. Put cookies into preheated oven and bake about 10 to 12 minutes, or until they turn light brown. Remove from oven. If they feel too soft, leave them on the sheet for a minute or so until they harden a bit and slide off the sheet easily.

Thanks, Bea.

ELEVEN

Trelawney

✤

Trelawney of the "Wells" was written in 1898 by Sir Arthur Wing Pinero. It's a sentimental comedy about a provincial repertory theater in Tunbridge Wells, England. It is a play about actors. So those of us lucky enough to be in the revival of this wonderful play had the opportunity to give the world at large an impression of ourselves. We were actors playing actors. We trotted out our foibles for all the world to see — the egomania, the self-absorption, and the self-indulgences; and also the in-genuousness, the empathy, the quest for the understanding of human nature that actors must have if they are to ply their craft. As some wise person said, "Actors are people, only more so." And we got the chance to show that every night in Trelawney.

It was a huge opportunity for me. It came as a result of my first leading role in New York, which was in Comedy of Errors in Central Park. I managed to catch Joe Papp's attention with that performance, and it happened right at the time he was casting Trelawney, which was to open his season at Lincoln Center. He asked A. J. Antoon, who would be directing the show, to drop by the Park and take a look at me. A. J. was Papp's hottest director, after having directed award-winning productions of *All's Well That Ends Well* and *That Championship Season,* both of which were successfully transferred to Broadway. After auditioning three times for A. J. and at least four times for Papp over a period of two weeks, I remember standing there on the empty stage while they whispered about me out in the audience. Finally Papp walked away from A. J., looked at me standing on the stage, paused, and said loudly, "Let the kid play the part." Then he smiled at me and left. That was the warmest moment I ever had with Joe Papp.

Not only was I playing one of the leading roles, but it was also my first chance at a romantic lead — I actually got the girl. One of them, anyway. I was secretly in love with Trelawney (played by Mary Beth Hurt), and Jenny (played by Meryl Streep) was secretly in love with me. Not a bad situation for a little Jewish boy from Baltimore.

And there was John Lithgow, fresh from his Tony Award–winning performance in *The Changing Room;* there was Mandy Patinkin; there was Jerry Dempsey and Sasha von Scherler and Jeffrey Jones and damn near every wonderful character actor in New York. And Christopher Hewitt. Chris and I had done a play together a year or so before. It was *The Rivals* by Richard Brinsley Sheridan, and Chris had played the leading role. I had one of the smaller, supporting parts. Now suddenly the roles were reversed and Chris was supporting me. He handled this as graciously as an actor could, insisting that I share a dressing room with him so that he could mother me through the whole process with a steady diet of hot tea and English good sense. There was Walter Able and Aline McMahon playing the grandfather and the maiden aunt. They were both well into their seventies and added the necessary ballast for the company. I was in actor heaven. This was my big break. It's a funny thing about big breaks — they're not about what comes after, not about what they get you. I learned that in *Trelawney*. It didn't matter if it led to another play or a film career or some award; it only mattered that what I was doing at that moment was everything I had ever wanted to do in my career. I was where I wanted to be — that's a big break.

Trelawney was a love fest. We loved the play; we loved each other; we loved ourselves — it was sickening. We sang together all the time. It started when we learned "Ever of Thee I'm Fondly Dreaming," which was sung during the play in the first act, and then again at curtain call. Peter Link wrote the beautiful music that lingers in my mind to this day. When we realized how good we sounded together, we started singing madrigals in the dressing rooms between acts. There were some first-rate voices among us, and the sounds were positively angelic.

Rehearsals always begin with the actors tying up the loose ends of their lives and their careers. Everyone is on the phone with an agent or a baby-sitter, and the whole company's focus is split between the outside world and the play. Then by the end of the first week, the outside world begins to fade into the background and a sort of communal delusion takes over with each actor starting to approach the play and his role from the inside rather than the outside. We each begin to see the play only from the perspective of our own character — like the old actor in a production of *Hamlet* who when asked what the play is about says, "It's about this gravedigger, he's not happy with his life, his back is killing him, and then some prince comes by to give him a hard time. . . ." That's why we need a director — to gather all the threads together and make a whole cloth. *Trelawney*'s rehearsals were a stitch. We were all cracking each other up with our impressions of actors. There was a dinner scene in the first act that introduced the whole acting company of the "Wells" at once. We all gathered for a boardinghouse dinner, and as the food was passed around and was inhaled in what seemed a few seconds, each character had the chance to reveal himself. The "low" comic told terrible jokes ad nauseam; the leading man talked about himself as if everyone were interested in nothing else. Romantic flirtations flew around the table as fast as the food, and the whole pecking order of the company took shape before the audience's eyes. It was a terribly difficult scene to stage. We spent days robotically passing plates with the names of the different foods taped on them for identification. We spent one whole afternoon tracking the ham as it passed from one character to another so that the plate could end up empty at exactly the right moment to get a big laugh from the audience. It was a painstaking procedure.

One day we took a break for lunch and the whole company went out to a deli together. We got a big table in the back, ordered a ton of food, and started passing it around. Somebody told a joke that convulsed the whole table. Then another actor started talking about a film offer, and another started a flirtation across the table. Suddenly, unconsciously, we were playing the dinner scene in real life — with the perfect controlled chaos, the laughter, the silent, secret heartbreaks, and the ravenous, actorly appetites. I saw A. J. sitting off to the side with a perplexed grin on his face, wondering if he could ever transport this madness to the stage. It took four more weeks, but he did.

A. J. orchestrated this community — onstage and off. After rehearsals, in the evening, he and I would cook for what became the special "in" group — A. J., Mary Beth, Meryl, Mandy, John, and me. A. J. and I had a great time cooking together, and the rest of the group had no trouble putting it away. His tastes ran to the ornate, while mine, as you know by now, are more basic. But somehow they blended well. We combined forces on a beef Wellington one night, with A. J. handling the pastry, and me the beef and duxelles. Rounded out with haricots verts and a few bottles of Château Margaux, it was an elegant dinner. Another night we would do Italian, with A. J. cooking a light risotto with zucchini and me weighing in with the main course of pollo scarpariello, or "shoemaker's chicken," which is the Napolitano's answer to fried chicken.

We were a funny group, each one of us out of balance in one way or another. John's marriage was creaking and would end less than a year later; Mary Beth was newly split from her husband, Bill. Meryl and Mandy were both fresh out of college and nervously facing their New York debuts; A. J. was immersed in the play, hiding from the fact that he had no ongoing relationships in the real world. I was on my own, Jill being in Washington with a play that was on its way to Broadway, and Alison shuttling back and forth between us. My feet were not on the ground. I was finally achieving the success I had wanted for so long and I felt alone and scared, not at all sure I could deliver on opening night.

We pulled together in the way that actors do. We made a communal, unspoken decision to suspend reality for a while; we made a pretend family of each other, replete with family-style meals to make us feel comfortable and at home. We blithely blinded ourselves to the inevitability that this family would dissolve on opening night and we would each have to work our way back into our real lives. Opening nights are exciting, but they do have a way of reminding you by the end of the evening that a play is just a play.

And our play was no exception. The reviews were mixed. Some were wonderful and said everything we wanted to hear about this play and production that we loved so much. But the *Times* was negative. Clive Barnes was doing the butchering for them in those days, and being English, he took offense at A. J.'s transplanting the play from England to turn-of-the-century New York. Anyway, he gave us the back of his hand.

We rallied; we reminded ourselves how wonderful we were and how much we loved each other, and we each took private satisfaction that the critic hadn't attacked any of us personally. We went on with the run. Then about a week later, the Sunday *Times* review came out, written by the éminence grisly of New York critics, Walter Kerr. I came into the dressing room after Saturday night curtain call and Chris Hewitt looked dolefully at me and said, "The Sunday *Times* is out. Don't read it." His meaning was clear; Kerr hadn't liked me. He had attacked my performance and perhaps me personally right there in print in the Sunday *New York Times* for all to see.

And I took Chris's advice. I didn't read it. It wasn't easy to walk away knowing that everyone else in the world knew what he had said about me except me, but I was strong. I decided that reading it would upset my equilibrium for the rest of the run of the show. I felt it was my responsibility to protect my performance. And I took solace in the fact that other people had loved me — even other critics — so I covered over the gaping hole in my stomach and went on with the show.

During the run I made a new friend — one who would have a great influence on me. Our friendship took shape backstage during the third act as we both waited to enter from stage right. Aline McMahon, who was playing the maiden aunt, had to tottle out on stage a few moments after my entrance. The third act took place in Trelawney's garret — an attic room supposedly up four flights of stairs. So, as I waited offstage to enter, I jumped up and down to flush my cheeks to make it seem that I had just run up all those stairs. Aline sat quietly in a chair, waiting for her entrance and watching me bounce up and down like a yo-yo. Then one night she motioned me over to her chair to whisper to me.

"Not here, darling. Out there." And she pointed out to the stage.

Now, what she meant by this was that all this bouncing around offstage was fine, but you still had to go out and act. It's when you get to the stage, in the light, that you have to come across with the goods. And every night she showed me what she meant. She quietly rose from her chair, entered the stage, and transformed herself into an out-of-breath dowager who had just climbed four flights of stairs and was not at all happy about it. Acting, it's called. It's not the bouncing you do offstage but the leap you take onstage — a leap of faith in your own ability. It comes with time and lots of experience.

Anyway, Aline decided to adopt me. She thought I was cute. And the attraction was mutual. Whereas she was fascinated by this young actor at the beginning of his career with all his dreams before him, I was drawn to the fact that she had seen it all and done it all and was still as enthusiastic and dewy-eyed as if she were twenty. We ended up spending a lot of time together. When others were flirting or starting intrigues, which were rampant in that particular company, Aline and I would chat over tea in her dressing room. The fifty or so years' difference in our ages melted away as we discovered areas of mutual passion. We talked a lot about philosophy and modern fiction; we spent hours talking about our respective marriages — her husband had died some fifteen years before, but he seemed very much alive when she talked about him. And we talked about wine — a topic we both felt we were authorities on.

We decided to have a wine tasting. She invited me up to her wonderful apartment on Central Park West on a Monday afternoon, which was our day off. Jill and Alison were still in Washington, so I was rattling around without direction, without obligation, without anchor. It was raining hard, a cold autumn rain, and I ran from the wine store to Aline's apartment and got soaking wet in the process.

"Sit by the fire and dry off," she said.

And I did, looking around at the furnishings, the art on the walls, the mementos of a full and successful life. Her husband had been a world-renowned architect. They had traveled the world, building whole cities where none had existed before. Between his career and hers in Hollywood, they experienced everything the world had to offer and met everyone that was interesting to know. "This is the world I want to live in," I thought. "This world of exquisite choices."

She put out crackers and cheese and a little pâté to have with the wine. I opened her bottle first — a young Riesling, just old enough to drink. It was perfect — unabashedly young, with a fresh, almost effervescent quality that surprised with each new sampling, a bell-like clarity — what wine folks call "round," which means it has no second or third tastes complicating the original impression. This wine was young and proud of it. It had no respect whatever for the pretension or weighty pomposity that comes with age.

I opened my bottle to let it breathe while we drank the Riesling and watched the rain. I had brought a '61 Château Latour, as venerable, weighty, and complicated a wine as money could buy. Aline smiled at me and shook her head.

"When we lived in Hollywood in the thirties, I was making twenty thousand dollars a week when I worked — which was quite often. We had a little house in the hills with a beautiful flower garden that we rented for forty dollars a month. We used to say we were stealing life."

I watched as she traveled back — some forty or fifty years

before — to when she was young and powerful and immune to time. Her face reflected a wonderment, a bemusement at how fortunate she had been. And how fortunate she felt she still was.

I went to the sideboard and got two clean glasses. I poured the Latour and we tasted. Then we tasted again. It was powerful and rich and velvety, with subtleties that slowly revealed themselves with each new taste. She laughed out loud and actually slapped her knee — a gesture that I hadn't seen since those old movies she had been in.

"Oh, you paid a pretty penny for this beauty!" I had, and it was worth it.

She asked me about my life with Jill, and I told her the whole story. About our beginnings and the turmoil created by the disparities in our careers. She nodded as if she had seen all those problems and respected their power.

"Just love each day," she said softly.

I couldn't tell whether she meant that we should love each other each day, or that we should love each day as if it were the first. Then when she flashed her broad, toothy, Cheshire cat smile at me, I knew she meant both. She was teaching me the same lesson again, the one I learned backstage. That art is in the doing — not the thinking or the planning. Make it fresh each time and don't muck it up with what you know. Then you have a chance to see what's really there.

"I'll try," I said.

"You'll be fine."

And then she raised a glass to toast what we had learned, to each other, to the afternoon. We clinked glasses, hers filled with red, mine with white, and we watched the rain.

Jill came to New York with her play about midway through the run of *Trelawney.* She was doing *Summer Brave,* a reworking of *Pic-*

nic by William Inge. It had run at the Kennedy Center in Washington for eight weeks and would now take its shot at a commercial run on Broadway. The moment she got back in town, it was clear to me that she was paying her toll and heading straight into the tunnel from which I had just emerged. Just as I was clearing my head from the potent dose of reality I had swallowed on my opening night, she was putting her blinders on, falling heedlessly in love — with her play, her character, and her new family — so that the play was no longer a play but a personal, familial event that had to be nurtured, pampered, and protected.

Being on the outside, and being a bit jealous that her passion was directed at something other than me, I watched from a vantage point similar to the critics' — from a cold, clear, realistic point of view, as opposed to the wet, messy place that Jill was headed into. I watched the opening night and thought the play wasn't particularly good; I watched as the critics agreed and crushed it with glee. It closed in one night. And then I watched as Jill cleaned out her dressing room, bringing home the bouquets of roses, most of which hadn't even fully opened yet.

So, which of these perspectives is more real? The cold place where you can see clearly, without emotions to cloud your sight, or the sloppy, intuitive place where you fall in love and go blind and bruise yourself — and then heal and fall all over again? I guess the question answers itself. At least for me. And Jill. And all the people I love.

Trelawney was a set run — twelve weeks, sold out to a subscription audience at Lincoln Center no matter whether it was successful with the critics or not. So we were protected from the ax, so to speak. We had settled into a wonderful ensemble experience in which we grew with and into the play each night. We had survived the trauma of opening and got back to the business of acting. And Jill and Alison and I were together; the family was intact again. Jill recovered from her closing and was already looking forward to her next venture, so our career situation was relatively balanced and healthy. All was good.

Some old friends from our Washington, D.C., days came up to visit and to see *Trelawney* on the last weekend of its run. They caught the Saturday night show, and the next morning we were all eating a leisurely brunch before I went off to do the final performance that afternoon. They had loved the show and spent the brunch gushing about it in glorious detail. Jim is an intellectual who at that time was working for a think tank; his penchant for wringing every last drop of analytical information from a subject was legend among us, and that day was no exception. He went on about the play in its historical context, and then he minutely dissected the production — from the casting to the costumes, from the music to the cast bios in the program. He was exhaustive, as always. But, he had loved the play, so I didn't mind.

And then, just before I got up to go, he said, "And your character was beautifully drawn. I couldn't have disagreed more with Walter Kerr when he said . . ." and then he went on to quote verbatim everything that Walter Kerr had said about me in his review. I sat there with a piece of bagel in my hand and my jaw lying on my plate. My face flushed, my fists clenched in anger, my heart pounded in my ears. I felt defensive and panicked and humiliated all at once.

"He said WHAT?" I screamed inside my head.

And Jim went on and on, now discoursing on some other aspect of the play, but I couldn't hear him. I looked across the table at Jill, who knew what I was feeling. The look on her face said that she would do anything to stop me from hurting. But there was nothing to be done.

The review wasn't even that bad. I mean, Kerr didn't ban me from the profession or anything; the acting police didn't come and take me away. But he had watched me from his cold place and he didn't like me — which is his prerogative. But I resented the fact that he had the power to barge uninvited into my performance, knock all the furniture over, and then just leave, without a moment's thought to the devastation he had wrought. Anyway, he ruined my last show. I couldn't get him out of my mind.

The experience of *Trelawney* was so strong that many of us stayed in touch. Meryl and Mary Beth and Lithgow are among our dearest friends to this day. But somehow I lost touch with A. J. He disappeared for a while. The critics were toughest on him, and he couldn't shake their scorn. Perhaps this was because they had been so lavish in their praise of him in earlier productions, and having believed them on the way up, he couldn't ignore them when they turned on him. His career took a tailspin; Joe Papp lost interest and went on to his next fair-haired boy. A. J. found it more difficult to get plays that he liked. I saw his name pop up here and there in connection with a regional theater production or something out of town trying to come in, but nothing that we ever got a chance to see.

Years passed and we moved to L.A. and I had all but lost track of A. J., when out of the blue he called.

"Still cooking?" he asked in that impish way of his.

Hearing his voice took me instantly back to *Trelawney*. The music, the madrigals, the impossible expectations, the friendships, the pride we had in our beautiful play. It was *the* production of my youth, and it swam in front of my eyes as I held the phone.

"I want to take you guys out to dinner — or are you too famous now?"

"No. Come over. We'll cook."

And he came. We cooked the old dishes — pollo scarpariello, risotto with zucchini, our famous green beans, tossed in much too much butter. Oh, I had forgotten how much fun A. J. was to cook with! We laughed, we dropped things, we made instant repairs. I had forgotten how much he liked to taste things as they were cooking. I had to defend the chicken with a chef's fork or there wouldn't have been enough left to serve everyone else.

He focused a lot of attention that evening on my son, Max, who was about ten years old at the time. He listened as Max played the piano, which he does brilliantly, and told him stories of pieces that he had played as a child. He played one silly song over and over and had us all — Max especially — screaming with laughter.

We talked about the old days and the special time we'd had with *Trelawney.* But Jill and I were aware of a new quality in A. J. Time and hard knocks had mellowed him. He was more interested in looking out, less obsessed with himself than before, less tortured. He stayed late. We seemed to cover everything and everybody that we all had in common. When he left we hugged, and the emotion I felt from him was powerful. We promised not to let so much time pass, and he left.

Four months later, A. J. was dead from AIDS. He hadn't wanted anyone to know. He had said good-bye to his friends in his way — personally and simply.

I was standing with a phone in my hand when I heard the news, and an image flooded my eyes. We were all standing on the stage of the Vivian Beaumont Theater at Lincoln Center. It was a rehearsal just before the first preview that night. A. J. had just staged the curtain call and we were all stretched across the huge stage, holding hands after the last company bow. Then the piano-roll music swelled up from the speakers and we all faced the audience — which at that point was just A. J., sitting alone

in the center of the house — and we sang to him. "Ever of thee,
I'm fondly dreaming . . ."

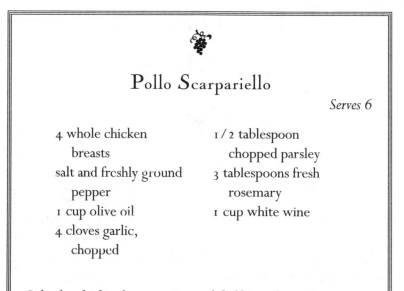

Pollo Scarpariello

Serves 6

4 whole chicken
   breasts
salt and freshly ground
   pepper
1 cup olive oil
4 cloves garlic,
   chopped

1 / 2 tablespoon
   chopped parsley
3 tablespoons fresh
   rosemary
1 cup white wine

Split the chicken breasts. Cut each half into three pieces, leaving the skin and bone intact. These should be large bite-size pieces. Season with salt and pepper.

Heat the oil in a large skillet until very hot and sauté the pieces until they're golden on both sides. This should take no more than 10 minutes. Then add the garlic, being very careful not to let it burn. Add parsley and rosemary.

Remove the pan from the heat and pour in the wine. Put it back over low heat and scrape up all the stuck-on bits.

Cook over low heat about 10 more minutes. Serve, pouring the pan juices over the chicken.

TWELVE

Italy – Then, Now, and Always

My Italian connection all started with a production of *Comedy of Errors* in Central Park. John Pasquin, who directed the show, decided to place it in a little Italian seaside village, turning Shakespeare's mistaken-identity comedy into a 1920s comic-mafioso family farce. The cast (which included the then-unknowns Blair Brown, June Gable, Linda Lavin, Roxanne Hart, Jeffrey Jones, Danny DeVito, Ted Danson, Don Scardino, and many others) learned broad Italian accents, gestures included, to fit into Shakespeare's decidedly English cadences. The results were hilarious. Literally spinning on Santo Loquasto's hundred-door set, we had one of the best experiences of our theatrical lives.

Comedy marked a turning point for me. I played my first leading role in New York and was successful. Whatever stigma the city had left on me was gone. That's not to say that I would never have trouble getting a job again — quite the contrary. But the days of being intimidated by New York were over. I could play with the big boys; I wouldn't always win, but I was in the game.

A few weeks after the show closed, I got a call from the American distributors of *Swept Away,* Lina Wertmuller's immensely popular comedy, asking me to audition for the job of dubbing Giancarlo Giannini into English for the broad American release of the film. They had seen *Comedy of Errors* and thought I had a good ear for the dialect. I got the job, and *Swept Away* led to *Seven Beauties* and then to dozens of other foreign-language films that I dubbed into English. It was yet another way to subsidize my theater career, which could always use a little help.

Months later I was reading a bedtime story to Alison when the phone rang. I heard a broad, almost comic Italian accent on the other end. I was sure it was Donny Scardino pulling a practical joke: "Dis isa Harry Colombo. I ama Lina Wertmuller's producer. Coulda you come-a to Roma to work witha her on the nexta picture?" I was in shock. Whereas my theater career was doing okay, I couldn't get arrested in the movie business. I thought this could be a big break for me.

And so began one of the more interesting journeys of my life. I was off to Rome for what became the better part of a year — to learn the movie business, "Italian style"; to meet friends who would stay with me the rest of my life; and to capture some of the secrets of Italian cooking, which I believe to be the most emotional, most soul-satisfying in the world. The memories flood into my mind — in no particular order, of course. Let's begin with an appetizer. It doesn't fit into the story at the beginning, but it's perhaps the best starter to a meal I know.

Roasted Peppers on Crusty Bread with Bagna Cauda

Serves 6 as an appetizer

8 sweet red or yellow
   peppers, or some of
   both
4 tablespoons butter
1 cup olive oil

4 cloves garlic, very
   finely minced
2 tins flat anchovies,
   chopped
crusty bread

Char the peppers on top of the stove until blackened; put them into a paper bag and close tightly.

Meanwhile, make the bagna cauda: Melt the butter and oil together in a small heavy saucepan — enameled cast-iron is best. Work over a low heat, as the bagna cauda can burn easily. Some people actually use a double boiler, but just being slow and attentive will do the trick. Sauté the garlic briefly, being careful not to let it take on any color, or it will turn bitter. Add the anchovies and mash them into a paste in the garlic, butter, and oil. Let the "hot bath" come together slowly until the aroma insists that you dip some bread into it. At that point, it's ready.

Remove the charred skins from the peppers, then seed and derib them. Cut them into the same size as your pieces of crusty bread.

Keep the bagna cauda warm over a chafing dish or fondue

candle when serving, or better yet, keep it warm on the stove and invite everybody into the kitchen. Use the bread to keep it stirred. Just dip the bread, add a pepper slice, dip it again and put it in your mouth. The second dip is crucial. There are few things better in life.

<p>

Meanwhile, back to Rome. Working with Lina was a complicated experience. I won't say it was always bad, but suffice it to say that having survived it, actually succeeding and even becoming friends with her by the end, taught me I could handle pretty much anything this business has to offer.

We were at cross-purposes from the beginning. In my mind I was there to become a major international movie star, and she thought I was there to teach pronunciation to her already-acknowledged major international movie star. She also didn't want to admit that she spoke not a word of English and wasn't exactly sure how she was going to pull this movie off. Mostly, she hated the idea that I had some small amount of control over Giancarlo. I was essentially teaching him English, and he was an apt pupil. He has one of the quickest minds I've ever seen. He also knew that if he could master this new language, his career would open up to all Hollywood had to offer. This idea did not make Lina happy.

Every day in her house, the three of us would work on the script. Giancarlo would say the line "I'm *going* to the *store*" as we had worked on it, and Lina would say, "No! I'm going *to* the store." And I would say, "Lina, we don't say it like that." Whereupon she would scream "Stronzo!" (Italian for shithead) at the top of her lungs and remind me that *she* was the Academy Award nominee and that I was a nobody, an unemployed actor who was lucky to be working, and then she hit me with the script a few times.

Above all, she made it clear that if the English in the film was no good, it was all my fault. She repeated this over and over. It seemed to make her very happy to say it. It was at this point that my skin started to break out.

Giancarlo and I devised a plan. At night, after the sessions with Lina, we would practice in secret. Once he learned the thought structure and cadence of the line to the satisfaction of both of us, we would then practice a way to say it incorrectly for Lina, who would the next day be able to say how stupid *I* was, whereupon Giancarlo would say the line correctly and she could take credit for it.

But most important, in our late-night secret sessions, Giancarlo and I would go to the kitchen (which he called the chicken — he could never get those two words straight) and toss together some aglio-olio to get us through the night. It seems to be the traditional Italian midnight snack, and it eased us through some tough times.

Aglio-Olio Giannini

Serves 4

1 / 2 cup olive oil
6 cloves garlic,
   chopped
1 pound spaghetti
salt and freshly ground
   black pepper

crushed red pepper
   flakes
freshly grated pecorino
   cheese (optional)

Put a big kettle of water on to boil. This sauce can be made while you're waiting. Put the oil and garlic in a sauté pan over *very* low heat. When the garlic starts to take on color, take the pan off the heat. Cook the pasta al dente, mix it in a bowl with the oil and garlic, add salt, pepper, red pepper flakes, and grated pecorino cheese, if desired.

The only reason I kept my sanity during these rehearsal days was that Jill and Alison were in Rome with me. And when I would finally crawl back to the hotel, they were there to calm me down and remind me what a lucky break this was. Then Lina decided to take even that small island of sanity from me. Not only did she cast Jill in the movie, but she announced dramatically that it came to her in a dream that Alison had to play

the daughter. Now the whole family was off to the loony bin —
with no one left to save us.

The rehearsal period ended with Lina and me barely speaking, and the whole troupe packed off to Padula, a beautiful hill
town in Reggio Calabria, to begin shooting. We all stayed in a
rustic hotel across from the *certosa,* or monastery, where most
of the shooting took place. And it was there that we met the
Rotunno family. Peppino was the director of photography for
the picture, and he had brought along his wife, Graziolina, and
two of his daughters to protect him from the madness. Carmen, their youngest, was Alison's age, and through the children
the two families became good friends and are to this day. Graziolina is a superb painter in the "naïf" style and one of the best
cooks I know. Her paintings of Emilia-Romagna hang in our
dining room, and *Lola,* her arms cradled around a huge bowl of
tortellini, hangs in our house in Big Sur. The Rotunnos have
nourished us in many ways over the years.

At dawn the whole film army would collect for breakfast
in the large first-floor dining room of the hotel, and I remember one morning when a small flock of baby lambs scampered
through the front door and into the middle of the room.
Alison and Carmen ran up to them, all excited — it was like a
Disney movie, watching the kids pet these precious little lambs
as they bleated contentedly. Then Willie, a great bearded bear
of a man who was the unit production manager and a famous
Roman Communist, quietly came up to me and whispered,
"Don't let them get too attached to the abbacchio." This was
not a familiar word to me and I started to ask for a translation
when it suddenly occurred to me that the kids were petting
dinner.

Here is a recipe for abbacchio, which is technically baby lamb
not more than a month old. This is difficult if not impossible to

get in the States. So substitute the youngest lamb you can find — preferably milk fed — and don't tell your children how cute it was before it was food. It can be cooked a number of ways, but there is likely to be garlic and rosemary involved. Here's a simple recipe and one that's very close to my memory of that meal in Padula.

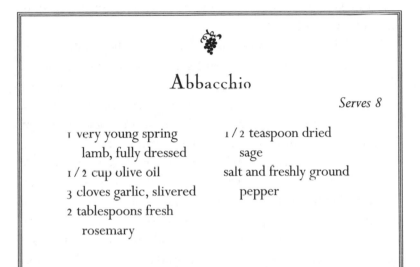

Abbacchio

Serves 8

1 very young spring
    lamb, fully dressed
1 / 2 cup olive oil
3 cloves garlic, slivered
2 tablespoons fresh
    rosemary

1 / 2 teaspoon dried
    sage
salt and freshly ground
    pepper

Combine the lamb with all the other ingredients and marinate for a few hours. Then roast it in a 400° oven until it is brown outside and tender inside (about 50 to 60 minutes, depending on the size of the lamb). Traditionally this is served at Easter with hard-boiled eggs and salami. The lamb can also be marinated in the same way, then roasted on a spit over hot coals. I prefer the latter method.

The shooting bumped along clumsily. Nothing seemed to be working. The English sounded like the dialogue from a Mexican porno film, and after each take Lina would look at me nervously, "This is how we say, yes?"

"No," I would mutter.

"Colpa tua!" she would shout for all to hear, "Your fault!" It didn't seem possible at the time, but I hoped, I prayed, that she could make a good movie out of this drivel. She was a genius, after all. The critics said so.

And if I thought things were bad then, they took a 180-degree turn for the worse when I started my acting part in the film. She knew this was where I was vulnerable — after all, I wanted to be a movie actor, not a dialogue coach. She knew this and she took me apart, surgically. My first line took more than forty takes to complete. She kept screaming things like "Terrible acting!" and "Ay, Dio! You ruin my film." After what seemed like hours, she made it clear to everyone that she was giving up; that this American idiot would never get it right; that I was blowing the entire budget of her film on this one line. Her derision was devastating and very, very loud. She wanted to make sure that no one in southern Italy missed a moment of my mortification. And then we would go on to the next line.

Giancarlo smiled his enigmatic smile and put his arm around me. "She really loves you, you know." Then he laughed and walked away.

By the time the whole crew moved to Rome to finish the picture in a studio there, Jill had returned to New York to start another job, and Alison had begun to shoot her scenes in the film. Lina was quick to point out that the daughter was far more gifted than the father and questioned her patrimony daily. She decided that I was to be barred from the set during the time Alison was to shoot. As I was leaving, I saw her grab my terrified seven-year-old by the shoulders, shake her, and scream, "Now I am your father *and* your mother!" Now I felt I had failed both as an actor and as a father. The crew felt for me and took me up above where the lights were hanging so that I could watch. And Alison nailed it — every time. She never did more than three takes, and Lina kept cooing, "Brillante! Magnifico! She's a jinius!" At least somebody in the family could cut it.

Then Alison finished, and she was gone too. I was alone. I remember leaving the sound stage every evening to walk the streets of Rome. We were shooting at Safa Palatino Studios on the ancient and beautiful Palatine Hill in the center of Rome. From there I would walk the eternally rain-soaked streets — me and the hookers — through Piazza Navona, through Campo Di Fiori, through the old Jewish ghetto near the Foro Romano, across the Tiber to Trastevere and my apartment. And I would stop, more often than not, at Ivo's, the great and venerable pizzeria, to drown my sorrows in mozzarella.

Eventually things got better; they couldn't have gotten much worse. Giancarlo took me aside and told me that Lina was making my part bigger and that all she really wanted was for me to stand up to her. So one day in the middle of a shot, when the camera was to pan over to me, I mooned her. A great big harvest-moon shot right in her face. She screamed. She loved it. She embraced me. She took me off to see dailies, which had previously been off-limits to me. She took the camera apart for me and explained the differences in the lenses. She was my friend — more, she was my mentor. If only I had known the power of my little Jewish butt, I could have saved myself a lot of grief.

That night after dailies, the inner circle, of which I was suddenly a part, went off to all'Amatriciana, a restaurant not far from Lina's house, where we ate that wonderful, famous pasta dish from the outskirts of Rome, drank young red wine, talked about the day's work, and yelled about politics. Willie, the Communist, excoriated Lina, the Socialist, while Tucker, the tourist, looked on — amazed that he understood almost everything being said, pleased that he was almost forgetting that Italian was a foreign tongue, frustrated that the movie wouldn't be made in this wonderful, expressive language in which these people were so eloquent and witty and subtle.

Suddenly Willie, who was deep into the grappa at this point, exploded at me, "You are not a Lithuanian Jew. Your parents have been lying to you. You are Sicilian!" Whereupon everyone toasted my new nationality and patted me on the back. Once again I was happy; I belonged. And the food and drink were again at the center of my happiness. I love this bacon-, onion-, and tomato-scented sauce. Ask my kids.

Bucatini all' Amatriciana

Serves 4

Traditionally, the sauce is supposed to be made with guanciale, which is a bacon made from the jowls of pigs. This doesn't show up too often on the shelves at the A&P. Even in Italy, pancetta is substituted most of the time. You can get an American version of pancetta in most Italian delis, and I use it sometimes, but often as not I break with tradition and use thick-cut American bacon. The taste is smokier but wonderful. Try it both ways. Also, over the years I've gone back and forth over the addition of garlic to the sauce. I recommend one finely minced clove, to add a little sweetness.

1 large onion, chopped
3 slices thick-cut bacon
   (or a similar amount
   of pancetta) cut into
   1-inch squares
2 tablespoons butter
2 tablespoons olive oil
1 clove garlic, finely
   chopped
1 (28-ounce) can im-
   ported San Marzano
   tomatoes, with half
   their juice

salt and freshly ground
   black pepper
crushed red pepper
   flakes
1 pound bucatini (or
   perciatelli or even
   penne)
freshly grated Parme-
   san or Romano
   cheese

Sauté the onion and bacon in the butter and olive oil until the bacon starts to look like something you would eat. Then add the garlic and sauté briefly. Add the tomatoes and break them up with a wooden spoon. Add salt, black pepper, and red pepper flakes to taste. The sauce should have a little kick to it. Let the sauce bubble away over a low to medium flame for a half hour or so, stirring occasionally until it comes together.

Meanwhile, boil water in a large kettle, salt it, add the pasta, and cook until it's al dente. Drain the pasta, put it in a bowl, and add the sauce. Cover with a few generous spoonfuls of the grated cheese and toss together.

Serve with more cheese on the table and extra red pepper flakes for those who like it hot.

჻

Later that year, in the late spring, Lina brought me back to Rome to participate in the dubbing of the film. I guess she didn't feel the English was muddled enough and she wanted to take another whack at it. One weekend Giancarlo's wife called and invited me to join her and the kids and some other friends for a trip south to the town of Fondi. They knew of my interest in things culinary, and Fondi is the home of the buffalo that make "la vera mozzarella" — the best in all of Italy. We would visit them and then go over to Sperlonga to swim in the sea and generally escape the heat of Rome. After a day of swimming in the Mediterranean and frolicking on the beach with the kids and their bare-breasted mothers and baby-sitters, buffalo were the furthest thing from my mind.

We ended up in a wonderful trattoria by the beach. I can't recall the name, but I remember every morsel I managed to cram into my mouth. All the ingredients for pleasure were there: the room was small and generating a powerful energy; it was a local hangout, not a tourist stop; and there was an easy, happy banter between the staff and the locals. The larger tables were filled with families; often four generations were represented around the table — great-grandparents on down to suckling babies — eating, arguing, and laughing.

Our table was in an expansive mood, the Italian friends easy with each other, the children's behavior forgiven by all but their own parents. I felt wonderful — warm from the day's sun, warm from the wine, far away from any responsibility. And the food kept coming: spaghetti with a sauce of tiny clams, garlic, parsley, and tomatoes — *never* any cheese! Then a fritto misto. I had never had this dish before, but it brought back memories of childhood crab feasts because of the presentation and the size of the portions — huge baskets lined with brown paper to absorb the oil, filled with fried things — calamari, shrimps, and little fish that we ate bones and all. Just when I thought I could eat no more, the main course arrived: fish, grilled to perfection. Three large platters were brought to the center of the table, each holding a whole fish that was large enough to eat us. I took a breath, squeezed lemon on top, and dove in. How do I do it? The answer lies in a piece of wisdom written on the wall of the bathroom in a little trattoria near Delphi: "Eat through the pain." Even though a lesser person would stop, even though you feel intense discomfort, if the food tastes good enough, there's always room for more. You can do it too. All it takes is practice.

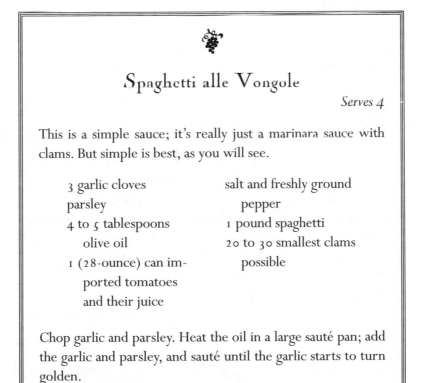

Spaghetti alle Vongole

Serves 4

This is a simple sauce; it's really just a marinara sauce with clams. But simple is best, as you will see.

3 garlic cloves
parsley
4 to 5 tablespoons
  olive oil
1 (28-ounce) can im-
  ported tomatoes
  and their juice

salt and freshly ground
  pepper
1 pound spaghetti
20 to 30 smallest clams
  possible

Chop garlic and parsley. Heat the oil in a large sauté pan; add the garlic and parsley, and sauté until the garlic starts to turn golden.

Add the tomatoes, breaking them up with a wooden spoon as they start to heat up. Add salt and pepper. Then slowly simmer the sauce for half an hour or so. Meanwhile boil water for pasta.

Scrub the clams and soak them in cold water while the pasta water is heating. When you add the spaghetti to the water, put the clams in the simmering sauce. They should open in about the time it takes to cook the pasta. If any of the shells don't open, remove them and discard.

Serve the pasta with the sauce and the clams in their shells. No cheese!

Jill and I finally worked up the courage to return to Italy about fifteen years after our Italian movie-business adventure. We figured that most of the people connected with our movie had either retired or gotten Alzheimer's or passed on to cinecitta heaven, so we could probably now cross the border undetected.

We called the Rotunnos to see if they would be around to spend some time with us. We had kept in touch with each other over the years and had spent a lot of time with them in New York and Los Angeles when Peppino was in the United States working on a film. Graziolina would always join him for at least part of the time, bringing her paints and canvases along.

When we called, it turned out that Peppino was doing a film somewhere in Europe, but Graziolina said she would meet us in Florence. She had spent her art-student days studying at the Uffizi and would love to guide us on a tour of her personal favorites. Jill thought this just meant art, but I knew she was referring to restaurants as well. She is one of the best cooks I know. She has a great knowledge of and pride in the cooking of Tuscany, where she lives part of the year, and Emilia-Romagna, where she was born. Besides being a "naïf" painter, she wrote to me recently, "I am a 'naïf' also cooking, so it is easier for me to cook than to write about food — because every time that I cook even the most usual food, I change something — it depends from many things — the sky, Peppino, or children, or il mal di pancia [stomachache] or maybe I have not the garlic and then I use the onion. But I really believe that so it is better."

I really believe that so it is better, too. Cooking must be intuitive. A recipe that was perfect on Monday must be changed on Tuesday because of those beautiful yellow peppers that showed up in the market, or because I'm a little blue and feel like adding some peperoncini to spice up my day, or a chicken that I wanted moist and succulent yesterday wants to be crisp and charred a bit today. Cook with your wants, not with your shoulds.

Graziolina met us at the hotel and whisked us off into Florence. Jill, who had been an art-history major in college, was now seeing not only the masterpieces she had doted on in school but also the city in which many of them had been painted. Graziolina knew all the stories and the political intrigues that surrounded the paintings and also filled us in on the technical aspects of the restorations that were going on in front of our eyes.

Then came lunch. We drove up to the little hill town of Fiesole that overlooked Florence and to a little *osteria* that Graziolina knew. It was raining, so we sat inside, missing the gardens and the view of Florence; but for me the view inside was even better. The room was full and warm and bustling. A fire crackled in the corner. The waiters were amiable, the crowd mildly boisterous. Everything pointed to a satisfying meal; I could just feel it. And the opening dish of pappa col pomodoro confirmed it. It was difficult for me to eschew pasta for my first course, but fortunately I wasn't given a choice. Bowls of the garlicky tomato-and-bread soup topped with a little green Tuscan olive oil went down beautifully on this brisk, rainy day, as soul-satisfying as the Botticelli paintings, as ancient as the Etruscan friezes, as simple and eloquent and perfect as the hand of Michelangelo's David.

Pappa col Pomodoro

Serves 4

1 1/2 pounds fresh tomatoes, peeled, seeded, and chopped

3 cloves garlic, thinly sliced

8 to 10 leaves fresh basil, roughly chopped

10 thick slices yesterday's crusty bread

10 cups vegetable broth

1/2 cup olive oil

Cook the tomatoes in a pot with the garlic and basil. Slice the bread and toast it, then add the toast and the vegetable broth to the pot with the tomatoes. Cover the pot and let the pappa boil until the liquid evaporates (the pappa should still be very soft). Drip a little olive oil over it. Serve hot or cold (I prefer hot). Graziolina says in her recipe, "It is very good for the little children."

The next day Graziolina gave us directions to Incisa, a little town just south of Florence where the Rotunnos' ancient villa and little farm were located. When I say ancient, I mean that the "new" section of the house was built in the 1400s. The old section, I didn't even want to ask. The kitchen was in the old part and is my favorite of any I've ever been in. It's large and centers around a huge hearth over which hangs a great black iron pot (still in use). There are all the modern conveniences one would need, but somehow you don't notice them. You focus instead on the old pine table in the middle of the room, the fireplace, the traditional cooking implements placed strategically around, the iron and copper pots and pans. And you focus on the painting above the sink, Graziolina's of course, of a traditional Christmas dinner, with the enormous family gathered around, the decorative Christmas breads in front of each place, and the bowl of tortellini in brodo as big as Lake Como in the center of the table. I have tried to buy that painting many times over the years, but no dice.

Graziolina cooked us lunch that day, and I can't remember ever enjoying a meal more. As always, it wasn't just the food — there were the people, the ambiance, the richness of the Tuscan hillside, the hospitality. But in this case, to be completely honest, it *was* the food. She decided to cook a meal from her farm — completely — perfectly fresh and perfectly local. The chicken was fresh-killed by her cousin Gianni that very day, the vegetables for the soup picked in front of our eyes, the butter, the oil, the wine, all came from within sight of where we ate.

Minestrone di Verdure

Serves 6

1 1/2 cups dry white
    beans
1 cup diced celery
1 cup thinly sliced
    onions
1 cup diced carrots
1 cup diced beets
1 cup diced zucchini
3 cups shredded cab-
    bage (Cavolo nero
    cabbage, if available)

1/2 cup olive oil
salt
8 fresh leaves basil,
    roughly chopped
3 fresh tomatoes,
    1/2-inch dice
6 crusty bread slices
Parmesan cheese

Put the beans in cold water to cover for one day; the next day, boil them until they are soft. Save the water. Cut all the vegetables into soup-size pieces. Lightly sauté the celery, onions, and carrots in the olive oil; as soon as they are a little brown, add the other vegetables. Add salt, basil, and tomato pieces; sauté for five minutes, then add the water that you cooked the beans in. Cover the pot. Simmer for 15 minutes or so, then add the beans and let them simmer with the vegetables for a half hour. Remember to stir with a wooden spoon on a fairly regular basis.

Toast the bread slices; put them in a soup tureen and pour the vegetables and broth over. Serve with a little Parmesan cheese, or just drizzle a little olive oil over the top.

Pollo alla Romana

Serves 4

1 (3 1/2-pound) fresh
   chicken, cut in
   pieces
2 tablespoons olive oil
1 clove garlic, thinly
   sliced

1 glass white wine
salt and freshly ground
   pepper
5 ripe tomatoes,
   chopped

Brown the chicken in the oil. Add the garlic, and when it is
golden, add the wine. When all the wine has evaporated, add
salt and pepper and the tomatoes. Cover the pot and let the
chicken cook slowly for about 45 to 60 minutes (depending
on how big the chicken is; remember, the small ones are
tastier).

THIRTEEN

Kerhonkson

Not all meals are notable because they're good. Some of the most intense cooking memories I have are of colossal disasters — huge culinary mortifications that still haunt my dreams. It has been said that you're not really an actor until you get laughed off the stage — God, what a horrible thought. So perhaps you're not a real cook until you've lived through a flat-out fiasco like having your oven break down ten minutes before you start cooking Thanksgiving dinner for twenty-two people (which has happened to me). All of which puts me in mind of the Great Seafood Disaster of '81.

We were up at our country house in Kerhonkson, New York, and we had invited Ron Schectman and Lynn Meadow over for dinner. Lynn was an old school chum of Jill's and the artistic director of the Manhattan Theater Club. She and Ron had recently gotten married and were staying up at their country place only a few miles away. The dinner was to be a casual, drop-in kind of event, mostly just to talk and drink wine and get to know each other. Then, a few days before, Ron called and asked if they could bring David and Susan Liederman along. Ron was David's attorney and an old friend of Susan's, and he said they were going to be in the neighborhood and that David wanted to taste my cooking again.

This changed everything. What was supposed to be a casual dinner was suddenly looming as a tension-filled test of my culinary abilities. David was a famous foodie, a restaurateur and cookbook writer. I had cooked for him a few times before in New York with some success, because he liked to eat the same way I did — as if each meal were his last on earth. But he made me nervous; cooking for him carried with it an implicit challenge, a test of my manhood   or of my whisking skills, to say the least.

I chose a recipe from Alice Waters's *Chez Panisse Cooking*. It was mixed seafood — mostly lobster, shrimp, and scallops on skewers, marinated in wine-butter sauce and grilled over charcoal — simple and great. It wouldn't seem as if I were showing off, but it would impress nonetheless. I'd put it together with a fresh garden salad and home-baked bread, and David would proclaim me a rustic, untutored genius.

The problems started with the wine. Susan was the oenophile of the Liederman family; she was in charge of stocking the wine cellar at their restaurant and really knew her way around the sniffing of a cork. She brought a case of great red wine — six Bordeaux and six burgundies — so that we could have a tasting. This was all well and good, but it was seriously screwing up my timing at the old charcoal grill. By the time I staggered out to the porch, where I had set up the Weber, it was well past nine o'clock and the only light was coming from a dim little porch lamp over by the door. I brought a flashlight out and tried to hold it in my teeth while using both hands to delicately turn the seafood on the grill. So far, so good.

Now, the secret of all seafood is not to overcook it. In one split second it can turn from a tasty, toothsome, succulent morsel to something resembling a Spaldeen, which for those of you who didn't grow up on the East Coast in the fifties is a little rubber ball that we used to bounce off the front stoop in a game called step-ball. Anyway, a Spaldeen is nothing that you would ever want to put in your mouth. So, working quickly and delicately, testing the springiness of each piece with my finger, being careful not to bite through the flashlight in my excitement, I transferred the finished seafood to a waiting, prewarmed platter that I had delicately balanced on the porch railing next to the grill.

I don't know whether I should blame my nervousness or the bottle and a half of Château Lynch-Bages that I had slugged down, but when I turned to put the last of the skewered seafood, just lifted from the grill with kitchen tongs and charred fingers, onto the waiting platter, I couldn't help but notice that the platter was not waiting. I looked around, using my teeth to focus the flashlight on various places on the porch that I might have set it down. Nothing. I had one of those moments where all time and space seem to melt into a huge, goopy marshmallow and you literally don't know where to go or what to do. You just stand there with the last skewer of seafood in your hands and a flashlight in your mouth and your eyes nervously darting around the porch. I remember hearing rollicking laughter from inside the house as the group drank and expectantly waited for their food.

Finally I set the skewer down on the porch, not wanting to put it back on the grill for fear of overcooking the seafood, and took stock of my situation. I knew where the platter was — barring some unseen intervention from alien beings from space — it had fallen down onto the lawn. Now, let me explain about the lawn. We had a goat named Mehitabel who lived down on the lawn. We bought Mehitabel to eat the grass after we fenced out the cows. Well, I guess I should explain about the cows.

Our property was in the middle of a dairy farm. We bought it from the buxom farmer's daughter   – whom we referred to as the dairy heiress — and her husband, an ex–prison guard, who had gotten divorced over trying to build a house from one of those log kits. We inherited the unfinished shell of the house along with all their frustration when we bought the property. Anyway, there we were in the middle of a dairy farm, and the cows were picturesque and all — from a distance. But up close and personal, they were stupid and smelly, and frankly a little intimidating. Plus they had turned our vegetable garden into what looked like Dresden after the bombing. So we asked the farmer to fence them out. But then the grass started to get out of hand, to the degree that our place looked abandoned. And it wasn't the kind of grass you could cut with a mower — there were big rocks and deep ruts and trees; it was a field, not a lawn. So we bought the goat. But for some reason, Mehitabel didn't eat the grass. She ate Alison's science project and things like that, and she often ran away, and she pooped a lot, but she wasn't interested in the grass. Anyway, this was the lawn that the seafood fell onto.

What was the best way to play this? I could come clean, admit the disaster, and go out for pizza. I knew David liked pizza. Or I could attempt a cover-up — I had often seen Julia Child clean up something that had dropped into the garbage pail or onto the floor and pop it cheerfully back on the platter and serve it. If she could dissemble, so could I.

I found the platter first. It had bounced under the porch where we kept the woodpile. The skewers of seafood were not quite so easy to locate. Because of the grassophobic goat, the lawn was a good foot high and the skewers were hidden — like Easter eggs, nestled in the high grass. So, even with the flashlight, I had to use the touch method to find them — being very careful not to step on them. Crushed seafood would be even harder to explain.

I put my flashlight back between my trusty teeth and, one by one, brushed off the grass and dirt and other unidentified bits and pieces from the exquisitely cooked seafood (I couldn't help but notice as I brushed it off that the scallops and shrimps were firm to the touch, but resilient — I had turned them at exactly the right moment). I assembled the platter decoratively and carried it back up on the porch, where I brushed it all again with the butter and wine marinade. I took a breath, hoping for the best, and carried it into the dining room.

Fortunately, everyone was so drunk that I could have served what I had brushed off the seafood instead of the dish itself and no one would have noticed. David did have a quizzical look on his face and asked me two or three times what that special herb combination was, that extra little crunch. I just smiled secretively and downed another bottle of wine. The evening was a great success.

What was it about this house among the cows and goats that seemed to invite disaster? I think perhaps it was that we bought it at a very dicey moment in the progression of our relationship, shortly after I had returned from Italy and my disembowelment by Lina. I remember it first coming up at a coffee house on Bleeker Street near Sullivan. We were sitting at a sidewalk table, scarfing down Italian pastries with what was then the best espresso New York had to offer. We were soaking up the atmosphere of the old neighborhood, remembering back to our early days in New York, when we were scared and broke and unem-

ployed. We were looking back in hopes of gaining a little perspective on our current career situation, which, although vastly
improved, was giving us fits in a different way. It was a simple
problem: Jill's movie career was taking off and mine was not.
Now, on one level I was perfectly sanguine about it because I
was a little gun-shy of movies after my experience in Italy,
and also this was a time when my theater career was bubbling
along rather nicely. I was working regularly in every institutional
theater in New York. From the Phoenix to the Roundabout to
the Manhattan Theater Club to the Second Stage, I was an inte-
gral part of nearly every forgettable play produced in New York
in the late seventies. So I rationalized that I would hold down
the legitimate-stage side of the family business while Jill sold
out to Hollywood. No problem, right?

But as much as I tried to convince myself of that, the reality
was that I lived in dread of her becoming a movie star. The hur-
ricane of attention she would get from the media, the sheer in-
equality of our respective careers in the eyes of the business and
the world, would blast our little love affair out of the water. I
was terrified that the world at large would discover what I had
known for years — that Jill could make you feel that you knew
her intimately and that she knew the best part of you. And I
didn't want to share that with the world at large or anybody
else. The sad, secret fact was that her love for me was a crucial
part of my self-image and I was terrified that it would seep
away. The irony of actors is that our egos are so large and so
fragile at the same time. And mine was showing some severe
stress cracks. "Who's that little guy standing next to Jill Eikenberry?" echoed in my fantasies, and not very far from reality.

Also there was the money aspect. The breadwinner aspect.
Like many enlightened husbands in those days, I was trying to
straddle the sexual revolution with one foot in the present and

one in the past — and this position tended to put the family jewels in a precarious situation. And it wasn't just me. As staunch a feminist as she was, Jill, too, had problems with being the primary wage earner. As much as we both believed in equal pay for equal work, deep in our psyches we were both uncomfortable with the man taking this secondary earning position. It would take many years and many flip-flops in our careers for us to let this old preconception die. Eventually, as we saw first Jill, then me take over the breadwinner's role — and watched it seesaw back and forth over the years — money lost its symbolic power. Finally it became just money.

We sat there on that summer day in the West Village, sipping espresso and nursing my bewildered ego, and Jill skewed the perspective again. As she has done countless times over the years, she changed the lens from close-up to wide-angle and took my mind off the small stuff and focused it on the infinite.

"I think we need trees."

It was a theme that had come up before. Although Jill loved the beach house, the starkness of the seashore left her yearning for the shade and protection and strength of trees. Big trees.

"We should look for our own place."

And, of course, this put the whole conundrum in a different light. Putting aside for a moment who earned it, this movie and TV money gave us the first real cushion we ever had. So, what better to do than promptly toss that cushion at the first big-ticket item that came along? Suddenly I had a role. If I couldn't be the earner, I would be the spender. I would hunt for our ideal spot, our haven from the world — our place with trees. Which would have been fine if it hadn't had that damn house on it.

There was always something off about this house, something unfinished. It had an aura that made my shoulders tense. Every time we drove up to it, I was shocked that it hadn't fallen down. Maybe it was the fact that we didn't really have enough money to support two residences. Or maybe it was because I wasn't the one who earned the money. Maybe it was just that I was never what you would call a handyman. But this house wasn't quite right when we bought it; it wasn't right when we finished it; and there was nothing anyone could do to make it right.

I remember another disaster that happened at the Cow Palace. And David Liederman was involved again — this time indirectly. He had cooked an incredible dinner for Susan's birthday, which we were fortunate enough to be a part of. Actually, I assisted him in the kitchen, doing highly skilled jobs like wiping off the counter, pouring wine, and taking out the garbage. But I did manage to watch him as he deftly boned a couple of ducks, stuffed them with a mixture of chestnuts and fruit and then sewed the stuffing into the ducks like a big, fat jelly roll, tied them with string, browned them, and eventually roasted them. Meanwhile, he took the bones, roasted them with vegetables, and put them into a stockpot to make a savory duck stock. All this happened in the blink of an eye as this 250-pounder danced around the kitchen like Gelsey Kirkland, his feet barely touching the ground. David transcends himself when he cooks — and I always learn something. Anyway, the crowning moment of this dish is when the stock, having reduced itself for hours, finally becomes this velvety glace de canard — savory essence of duck — and gets spooned over the perfectly roasted, boned, stuffed ducks.

So, six months later at Casa Disastro, I decide to recreate this dish for Christmas dinner. We were hosting Jill's mom and step-dad, who had flown in from Wisconsin, which meant the house was filled with that wonderful festive tension that only holidays with the relatives can give you. The fir trees were heavy with snow, the woodstoves crackling with fires, the electricity cutting out intermittently — it was Christmas in the country.

I must admit, I didn't bone the ducks. I had the butcher do it. He didn't want to because it was Christmas and he was busy, but I bribed him. For those of you who have never boned a duck, my advice is to bribe the butcher. You get two neat packages — one with the ducks, one with the bones — and you retain your sanity.

Anyway, things were bubbling along beautifully. The stock had been going for hours and was becoming deep and rich. I strained it and put it on a simmer to begin the reduction that would end up as the velvety, rich essence that I had loved so much at David and Susan's house. My ducks were all in a row, stuffed, rolled, tied, and browned, ready for the roasting pan. The house smelled like Paul Bocuse's kitchen, and all was right with the world.

With a dish like this, timing is everything. The ducks have to be roasted carefully and basted regularly, so that the stuffing warms as the flesh gets done just to perfection. Meanwhile, the reduction is reducing beautifully, getting richer, thicker, more essential. I call everyone to the table. I want to be sure that dinner is eaten when it's hot and perfect. Ralph, Jill's mom's husband, is prompt and eager, his napkin on his lap. Alison is in her chair, hungry and ready to go. And Jill and her mom are — gone. I call again; this time my voice has that little hint of threat, of accusation that it gets when I feel my cooking is underappreciated. They seem not to be in the house. I run back to my ducks — perfect. The reduction — ready. I run outside; perhaps they're on the porch. No. I run back to my ducks. They must come out now. I put them on top of the stove, cover them with tinfoil, and scream for Jill and her mom to come to the table. Then I see them out the window. They're in deep discussion about some wildflower or acorn or something and they're strolling nonchalantly toward the house. I run outside and beg them to come immediately. They smile and say that they are coming and that I shouldn't get all anxious and tense, because it's Christmas and we should be relaxed and happy. Steam comes out of my ears and I run back to check my reduction. It's gone. The pot is empty except for a little brown crust in the bottom. I have made the ultimate reduction. Six hours of careful pampering and simmering has resulted in what looks like a little booger in the bottom of my pot. I grab the pot in disbelief and promptly get a second-degree burn on my hand. Dinner was eaten in silence. To this day, Jill doesn't understand what she did wrong.

Not everything that happened in that house was bad. Max was conceived there. That was good. And to be honest, we had some good meals there, too. And a few great ones. There was a Labor Day picnic with just family and a few friends who had houses in the neighborhood — Steve Harrison and Claudette Sutherland came, and Judd Hirsch and his girlfriend. And we charcoal-broiled steaks, the best steaks I've ever had — and I've had my share. There's no great secret to a perfect steak. It happens in the shopping. And there's a butcher in Kingston who sells the best meat in the world. Better than all the vaunted Manhattan beef boutiques like Lobel's and Ottomanelli's, where the steak goes for more money per ounce than imported perfume. Not that Schneller's is cheap, mind you.

Schneller's butcher shop is on a small street in the old section of Kingston. It's been there for years. There's a little German restaurant upstairs — also called Schneller's — that's strangely quaint; it seems more for ladies having lunch while shopping downtown than for serious eaters. I tried it only once and had sauerbraten, which I have a soft spot for ever since my days in Milwaukee, and found it a bit ordinary — but the meat was first-rate. I didn't have a steak because I was only there for lunch, and a big steak at one in the afternoon would pretty much finish the day for me. And I like to cook my steak myself. That way I know I'm getting it the way I like it.

What is it about Schneller's beef that makes it so superior to any other I've tasted? I looked into it in depth because I've shopped steak from coast to coast, in the best butcher shops money can buy, and this is clearly the best. Local lore has it that the train carrying the beef from the midwest slaughter houses comes through Kingston on its way to New York, and Herr Schneller (or whoever's running the place these days) pulls off the best of the best before anybody else has a shot at it. Whether this is the case or not, it would certainly explain the mystery.

I'm not going to describe the steak to you. You all know what it looks like. I'm not going to say "marbled," because of course the steak was marbled; it was prime steak — super prime, if such a thing exists. Anyway, I had them cut thick sirloins — two and a half to three inches, at least. Maybe a touch more. You're going to cook it over very hot coals, so you want that thickness; then you can get a proper char on the outside while bringing it to the perfect red, juicy, almost pornographic pinkness on the inside. This is why you need steaks of the highest quality. The superabundance of fat inside will keep them properly juicy while you're torching the outside.

Brush the steaks with a little virgin olive oil — it pays to use really good olive oil. You don't use that much, and it makes a difference. And that's it. No salt. No pepper. No Worcestershire sauce. No soy sauce. Just a little oil — good oil — and make sure the steaks are at room temperature before you put them on the grill.

Sear the steaks on both sides; that means a minute or so on one side, then flip them to the other. I don't use a fork to do this because piercing the meat during cooking is a bad idea. Use tongs or two spatulas, or whatever you're comfortable with, but not something that pokes through the surface of the meat. I can't tell you how long to cook them. Each grill and each steak is different. You just have to get a feel for it. Touch them from time to time. When they start to resist a little, rather than just mush down, you're close. And watch them carefully. With a thick steak like this, you can see on the sides what's happening on the inside. This is a powerful argument for not grilling in the dark, which, as we have seen, is a fool's game.

When the steaks are done, let them rest on a preheated platter for five minutes or so. This lets all the juices return to the center of the meat. Then, there are two schools of thought: you can slice the steaks on the platter, letting the juices collect on the plate for later distribution, or you can put the whole steaks — on their platter — in the center of the table and let people slice their own. I recommend the former, because when the meat lust is high and you have all these people pushing to the center of the table at once, armed with steak knives and forks, it could be a bloodbath. So, avoid armed hostilities; slice at the counter. Cut the steaks against the grain, on the diagonal, about a half-inch thick. Lay the slices across the platter, spoon the juices over, *then* salt. Then serve. If the steak is really good — like the steak I used to get at Schneller's — you won't have enough. No matter how much you buy. It's a law of physics.

Here's the recipe for David's duck dinner. You may not get it right the first time, but it's worth trying again.

David's Duckies

Serves 4

1 / 2 pound chestnuts in the shell	1 (4-pound) duck, boned
1 1 / 2 cups (1 / 2 pound) dried, pitted prunes, cut into quarters	1 large onion
	3 tablespoons butter, plus extra for sauce, if needed
1 / 2 cup (2 ounces) dried apricots, cut into quarters	3 tablespoons tarragon champagne, or white wine vinegar
salt and freshly ground pepper	1 / 2 cup duck reduction
2 pounds McIntosh apples	2 tablespoons minced parsley

Cut the chestnuts in half vertically. Peel off the tough outer skin; the inner light brown skin will come off later.

Bring 2 cups of water to a boil. Parboil the chestnuts for 3 minutes (they should not begin to turn soft). Drain them and quickly peel off the light brown inner skin while they are still hot; otherwise it will not come off. Cut the halved chestnuts in half vertically again and put them in a mixing bowl.

Add the prunes and apricots. Season with 1 teaspoon salt

and 1/4 teaspoon pepper. Peel, core, and roughly dice the apples. Add them to the mixing bowl. Set the stuffing aside.

Preheat the oven to 500 degrees.

Rinse the boned duck and pat dry. Season the flesh side of the duck with salt and pepper and stuff the bird with as much stuffing as possible. Fold the sides of the duck around the stuffing and sew the open seam together to create a pocket for the stuffing. Season the outer skin with salt and pepper and prick the skin all over.

Place the duck in a heated roasting pan on its side and roast it for 10 minutes. Prick the skin again and turn the duck onto its other side. Roast for another 10 minutes. Prick the skin again and roast the duck, breast side up, for another 25 minutes.

Puree the onion in a food processor or mince it by hand and finish pureeing in a blender.

Melt 3 tablespoons of butter over low heat in a medium saucepan and sauté the pureed onion for 20 to 30 minutes, stirring occasionally, until mixture begins to turn light brown.

Add the vinegar to the puree and simmer for an additional 2 to 3 minutes. Add the duck reduction and bring the mixture back to a simmer. Turn off the heat.

If the duck is properly crisp on the outside, remove it from the oven and let it rest for 10 minutes.

Gently reduce the sauce while you slice the duck. Make sure to add all the pan drippings to the sauce. If you want the sauce to be richer, add more butter.

Adjust the sauce seasoning to taste. Pour the sauce over the sliced duck. Sprinkle chopped parsley over the duck.

*   *   *

For the duck reduction that's called for in this recipe, I refer you to any book on classic French cuisine or, more to the point, to David Liederman and Michèle Urvater's book, *Cooking the Nouvelle Cuisine in America,* published by Workman Publishing. And remember not to go looking for your wife and mother-in-law just before it's ready or you might have to send out for pizza.

ॐ

FOURTEEN

Ireland

❧

I've never much liked the telephone anyway, but the call I got that afternoon clinched it. I was at home alone, expecting a call from the assistant director of a movie I was shooting. I was the cover set, which meant that if it rained that day, my scene would work. And it looked to be clouding over. I was shooting the movie version of Herb Gardner's play *The Goodbye People,* which I had recently done on stage — in Westport, Connecticut, then in Los Angeles, and finally on Broadway at the Belasco Theater, where we closed after one performance. The brief run notwithstanding, I loved the play and was delighted to be a part of the movie.

"Mike . . ."

It was Liz's voice — my first wife. There was no question from the tone in her voice that bad news was coming. She almost whispered my name; and when she spoke it, it had that downward inflection, like something final, something dreadful.

Liz was traveling in Ireland with her father and Alison. It was school spring vacation, and Alison usually spent her vacations with Liz. This was to be a merry jaunt by horse-drawn caravan through the Dingle Peninsula in southern Ireland. They would camp out of the caravan and cook by the side of the road, and really experience the countryside firsthand.

"I don't know how to tell you this. . . ."

"Just tell me," I said flatly.

"Alison's been hit by a car. She's in a coma."

"How . . ."

And as I tried to formulate my first question, I lost it. My throat closed, and tears rushed out of my eyes, and it seemed as if I already knew everything. It seemed that I had known it all since the moment she was born. And all this time in between, I had just been waiting for it.

"Is she going to die?"

"They won't tell me anything. No. I don't think she's in mortal danger, but they have no idea . . ."

". . . how much damage has been done."

"Yes."

We let that sink in. "Look, there's no need for you to be here until she comes out of it."

"We'll come."

"Well." She sounded defensive. She always got that superior tone when she was off balance. "There's nothing to be done but wait."

"Then we'll wait."

She told me that they were in a hospital in Tralee, where the accident had taken place, and I told her we would try to come that night.

When I hung up, I was lost for what to do. Jill was in rehearsal downtown. I called and left a message for her. I found our passports, which had both expired, and I stood there holding them in my hand and walking around in a circle. Max, who was a year and a half old, was in the park with Veronica, his baby-sitter. I was desperately afraid something would happen to him — and to Jill — to anyone who wasn't with me, under my protection. Then I called Mary Flanagan. Somehow I knew she could put in motion what I could not. She listened, and then told me not to go anywhere and that she would call me right back. I waited.

A few minutes later, Jill called. I told her, and she was on her way. Veronica and Max came back from the park, and I asked Veronica to stay close. She asked if Max would be going and I said that he would. I didn't want anyone out of my sight. A few minutes later, Jill came through the door. When I saw her face, whatever muscle that had been holding me together let go. All our years together, from our first moments — from when I first told Jill that I couldn't leave my baby — Alison has been a part of us. And then when she was actually a part of us — when she switched mothers at a year and a half and moved in with us — we watched and waited for signs that this disruption would affect her. We nurtured her. We carried her along the way little children at the beach carry water, cupped in their two hands, carefully and slowly. And now, from three thousand miles away, the water was slipping out and I couldn't do anything to stop it. We held each other for a long time, drawing strength.

Mary and Marc showed up at the house. As Mary started to pack our bags, she told us the plan. She had contacted Henry and Stacy Winkler, which was, of course, the perfect thing to do. Henry, Jill, Marc, and Mary had all been together at Yale. And now that he was the king of television, he was as close and loyal to his friends as always. More so, if anything. And Stacy is, of all the people in the world, the one you would want next to you in a crisis. They had waved their magic wand and everything was in motion. The State Department had been called; our passports would be taken care of in Ireland. A limo pulled up and took us to Kennedy, where we had first-class tickets waiting for us. In a matter of a few hours, the three of us were flying across the ocean, in a stupor, not at all appreciating our first experience in first class.

We landed in London because it had been too late to book a direct flight to Shannon. We were met by an associate of Richard Grant's, Henry's publicist (years later to be ours as well), who gave us some money. All this had happened after the banks closed, and there were no ATM machines in those days. He gave us as much cash as he could spare and directed us to the flight to Shannon.

When we landed in Shannon, there was a message waiting for us that Alison had been moved by ambulance to Cork because the hospital there had more sophisticated equipment. The message said that her condition was the same. We gathered our bags and I went to rent a car. When I realized that the steering wheel was on the wrong side, I decided I was in no shape to negotiate the difference. I was tired, my nerves were shot, and I would have put the car smack into the first tree we came to. It crossed my mind that maybe this wrong-side-of-the-road business could have caused Alison's accident. We never found out.

I saw a group of taxi drivers standing together near the exit of the airport.

"Could anyone drive me to Cork?" One of the drivers raised his hand.

"Where would you be goin' in Cork?"

"The Cork Regional Hospital."

"And who would be in the hospital?"

I explained our situation and he told me to bring our bags up and he would get his car. Jill said that we needed to make one stop; the baby hadn't eaten all night and would need a little soup or something. He said that would be no problem, and that he would be right back with the car.

After we loaded the car, he drove us to his house. He had phoned ahead and his wife had soup and some sandwiches and hot tea all ready for us. We started to protest, but he just held up his hand and smiled.

"You need this," he said. "Then we'll be on our way."

Looking back on it from twelve years away, I want to remember that their house was a thatched cottage. But in all truth, I think it was a semidetached brick house in a very modest neighborhood of semidetached brick houses. It was that dark sand colored brick that you see so much of over there in the outskirts of the cities. But there was a fire. A turf fire.

They were very shy with us. It was as if they thought if they spoke too loudly or too often, we would break. And perhaps we would have. She served us tea and little sandwiches — mostly bread with a thin layer of some indeterminate canned spread; it was fish, or ham perhaps. I must say that Max had no problem with the sandwiches. He ripped through them like a born Irishman. And then she brought out large, piping bowls of oxtail soup that had been on the fire simmering for at least three generations. I will never forget that soup.

When you think about what food really is — sustenance, in the real sense of the word: corporeal, emotional, and even transcendent sustenance that feeds parts of us that were hungry long before we were even born — then I guess this soup was the best meal I had ever been fed. Not only because it was good — and it was powerfully good — but because the food, and the spirit with which it was offered, merged in that moment with our need for exactly that kind of food, served with exactly that kind of love. And, yes, it was love. Not the kind of love between friends or relatives, but a stranger's love, offered openly to people in need of it. Not much was said around that table. It wasn't the Algonquin. We were off to Cork so quickly that I can appreciate the moments we spent there more in retrospect than I could at the time. We never saw the taxi driver's wife again. He never left our side.

When we arrived at the hospital, he waited while we found Liz, who took us down to see Alison. When we found her, she was on a gurney, waiting to receive another brain scan. We stood and watched her in her suspended state for a long time. Liz and the doctor were talking, essentially saying that they knew nothing more. But I was focused on Alison in her comatose state. Where was she? I couldn't find her in there. Her soul or her essence wasn't there. I started to panic. I wanted to shake her, to make her appear. I remember, at that moment, kicking into a new level of fear; the adrenaline wouldn't stop pumping. Liz was suggesting we take round-the-clock shifts, so that one of us would be there when she came out of it. Then she recommended the bed-and-breakfast where she was staying, which was just a couple of blocks from the hospital.

Our taxi driver moved us to the bed-and-breakfast and asked if we needed him for anything else. By that time he seemed a member of the family. We said we were okay and got his address and phone number, and he was gone. Like a knight in shining armor or the Lone Ranger, he had appeared, performed his incredible acts of mercy, and ridden off into the sunset never to be heard from again. It turned out that he was only the first of many angels that we met in Ireland. They seemed to surround us.

We moved into our tiny room with two tiny wet beds, one for Max, one for Jill and me. Ireland is a wonderful country, but the beds are perpetually moist. Cold and moist. We unpacked. I sat on the edge of the bed and finally let other thoughts into my head. It suddenly occurred to me that I hadn't told the movie people that I had left the country. I went to a pay phone and called Herb. He was the writer as well as the director of the movie, and he was a good friend. I told him what had happened.

"Recast, Herb. I have no idea how long I'm going to be here. I'm sorry."

"We'll wait," he said.

And they did — for more than a month, which is not easy to do on a low-budget movie. Later that night we got a call from Barbara Sproul, Herb's wife. She's very active in Amnesty International and told us that she had a powerful friend in Ireland and if we needed anything — in terms of care from the hospital, or anything else — to call a number that she gave us. I put it in my wallet for later. All I needed at the moment was my daughter.

Two days later we got a call from the hospital at about five in the morning, "She's coming out of it!" We scooped up Max and ran to the hospital. Liz and many doctors and nurses were around her bed; the mood seemed high, expectant. I went to her bed and put my head next to hers.

"It's Daddy, honey, can you hear me? Bo?" That had been my name for her since she was a baby. Still is. "Can you hear me? It's Daddy."

She stirred; her eyes flickered and she said — almost inaudibly — "Barely." And I knew she would be all right. It was just a smart-ass enough reply to tell me that she was back. I could see her again.

We then started what would become a two-year recovery. It began with finding out about her other injuries, which we hadn't focused on yet. Her pelvis was shattered, and she had broken bones all over her body. They were loath to put her under any anesthetic because of her head injury, so we had to wait a couple of weeks for them to put her into a full-body cast. And we met the brain surgeon. In Ireland surgeons are called Mister rather than Doctor; it is a title of even more respect and power — primarily power. The waves parted when this guy came down the corridor. He strode into the room, obviously in a hurry, and looked into Alison's eyes. Then he turned to us and started describing the many dire possibilities that we could still discover about her condition. I asked him if we could discuss this outside — I didn't want Alison to hear all this negative talk — and he shrugged, went over to the wide-awake Alison, pulled down her lower lids and peered into her eyes again, and said, "She won't remember any of this." It was then that we realized how slow the recovery is from a brain injury. To this day Alison doesn't remember much of anything about her month and a half in Ireland.

Jill, Liz, and I continued our rotation on a twenty-four-hour basis, and Jill and I spelled each other with Max. Liz cut as wide a berth as possible around all of us. She wanted little to do with Max and even less to do with me. Her tension seemed to increase daily, until I thought she would implode. Not only was my family a constant reminder of our failed marriage, but her guilt over the accident was overwhelming her. She had been in charge; she was the temporary, "vacation" mother of her own child, and during her watch the unthinkable happened. I tried to be as nice and nonjudgmental as possible, which was exactly the wrong thing to do. It seemed to her to be patronizing and false, which I'm sure it was, because in all truth I believed that the accident wouldn't have happened if I had been there. There's no sense to this, but that's what I believed. The tension between us continued to mount.

Meanwhile, the situation with Max was getting more and

more difficult. He was a year and a half old and full of energy and curiosity. After a few days he had seen all of the hospital that he wanted to see, and we were looking forward to possibly months more of our vigil. We needed a baby-sitter. I remembered that number that Barbara Sproul had given me. She had said to call it if I needed anything, so I did.

"Sean MacBride's office. May I help you?"

Her voice was kind and her accent was right out of a Barry Fitzgerald movie.

"My name is Michael Tucker; I'm a friend of Barbara Sproul, who told me to . . ."

"Yes, Mr. Tucker. We've been expecting your call."

I explained our problem and she listened patiently. Then there was the slightest pause, and then, "Yes. A baby-sitter. Of course. Let me get back to you, all right?"

And in less than an hour she called back with a phone number of a Mrs. McGinnis, who she said lived only a few streets away from where we were staying. We called and Mrs. McGinnis invited us to come over. The three of us walked through the modest neighborhood until we came to the McGinnis address. The front yard was teeming with kids — seven or eight of them, at least, from the age of six months or so all the way to ten or eleven. We figured that Mrs. McGinnis ran a day-care center of some kind out of her house, which would be a fine situation for Max. But as we looked closer, the kids all looked the same — black Irish through and through. They all had midnight black hair and dark eyes and that beautiful, pale, milky complexion that seems almost translucent. They were definitely all from the same family.

As we walked through the gate, they made an excited circle around our little blond, curly-haired boy as their mother called to them from the porch.

"Now don't frighten the little lad. Give him space to breathe."

We were a little concerned that Max would have trouble staying with a stranger. He was in a very clingy stage — made worse by our vulnerable state of mind. Jill thought that perhaps she would have to stay with him for a time before he'd be comfortable.

"Oh, little darlin'," cooed Mrs. McGinnis as she unfolded her arms from her ample bosom and reached them out to Max. Without a moment's hesitation, he went to her and was immediately enfolded. The kids crowded around, enchanted by this cherubic little tot, who must have looked just like the angels they had seen at church. Max was in heaven. Mrs. McGinnis shooed us away, told us to go and tend to our daughter, and closed the gate behind us.

So, we had our baby-sitter. We were very grateful to the offices of . . . what was his name again? I fumbled in my wallet for the little piece of paper. Oh yes, Sean MacBride. What we didn't realize at the time was that Sean MacBride was the founder of Amnesty International and Ireland's only winner of the Nobel Peace Prize. That's who found us our baby-sitter. So if you're ever in Ireland and you don't know what to do with the kids, I have a number for you to call.

Our friends in the States kept funneling support to us. The Winklers and the Flanagans were in touch on almost a daily basis; Steven and Barbara Bochco found out about it through the grapevine and were a tremendous help. Meryl Streep, who had always been close to Alison since the *Trelawney* days, called from California the day before she won the Oscar. Our landlady at the bed-and-breakfast, who fielded the call, was properly impressed. David Liederman opened up a banking conduit through his business in New York so that we could draw whatever money we needed.

And the Irish people who surrounded us continued to display their remarkable generosity of spirit. The lady who ran the corner grocery called me over one day and said that if we needed milk early in the morning for that "darlin'" little boy, to check under a big bush to the left of the store where the milkman hid his delivery every morning before the store opened. "You can straighten up with me later," she said.

On my time off from the hospital, I walked around Cork. I think I had walked every inch of it by the time we left. The ancient stone streets smelled of burning coal, the smoke coming out of every house and covering the city with soot. I found a favorite pub, where I would sit off to the side and watch the men come in after a day's work. But it's hard to be a stranger in an Irish pub. You can't hide. So eventually they pulled my story out of me. I was Yank, with the little girl up at the "Regional."

"You need the right solicitor, Yank. Someone to take you through the twists and turns of the Irish system."

"At least she should come away with a little something for her future. After all that pain and suffering."

We sat and planned my legal strategy, and I alternated shots of Irish whiskey with glasses of Guinness. And I started smoking cigarettes again. Everybody smokes over there, and they have this way of offering you a cigarette each time they go into their pack. It didn't take long for me to start taking them. I had quit when Max was born; now that Alison had almost died, I started again. But, to be honest, it had nothing to do with my kids; it was totally self-centered. When confronted with my own mortality and the fragility of life, I felt a need not to deny myself anything. That was my first impulse. "Quick, before you die, drink everything, smoke everything, and above all, eat everything." Maybe that way, I thought, I could win the game before it ended.

By the time I tottered out of the bar, it was dark. The city streets took on a whole different tone — little houses with families tucked behind curtains, eating dinner together in front of the toasty coal fire. I walked the cold streets alone, fueled by whiskey, and listened to the sound of my shoes on the pavement. I went into a little Chinese take-out place — not so different from the one at Broadway and Ninety-third Street — and got cartons of food to take home. I hailed a cab so that the food wouldn't get cold. When I got there, I found that Liz was at home and Jill had gone over to the hospital with Max. I offered her some food.

"I really don't think that Mrs. O'Hara wants her parlor turned into a Chinese restaurant."

"She said it was okay to bring food in if we needed to."

"Well, I think you're taking advantage of her hospitality."

I was in no mood for a lecture from Liz. I was drunk and hungry. I sat down and started to eat from one of the cartons, turning my back to her.

"It's enough that that little boy runs around her house, breaking things."

I didn't want to take the bait, but she was pushing it. She must have known what she was doing. We hadn't been married for that long, but it was long enough for her to know where the buttons were. And she was getting dangerously close to the one that triggered the nuclear arsenal.

"I don't know why you haven't sent him home — to some grandparent or something. I don't understand why you thought you had to bring him in the first place."

I hurled the carton of prawns with lobster sauce at her head. My aim was off because I was seriously drunk, and it splattered on the wall behind her. Her voice went up a couple of octaves.

I couldn't understand what she was saying at that point, but it wasn't about fear. It was rage. She came at me with all the fury and frustration of a woman who had been abandoned and whose child had been taken from her. By me. I had done all this to her. And now I was blaming her for this accident. Her eyes lit up with an almost ecstatic look as she came at me, spitting her furious barbs, taunting me. I think, really, that she wanted me to kill her at that moment. And I was inclined to oblige her.

Thank God I'm not a killer, I'm a screamer. We vented at each other for what seemed like hours, until we were exhausted. Then we cleaned the Chinese food off the wall. And we even ate a little, I think. Not off the wall, but the other stuff. I think that moment finally ended our marriage for her. She let go of some things that had been festering for a long time. And we became just people who had a common interest — our daughter. I can't say that was the finest meal I ever ate, but the beef with broccoli wasn't all that bad.

When I visited Alison at the hospital, I would bring her some burgers and fries and a chocolate shake from an Irish version of an American fast-food restaurant. It made her yearn for the States, for her friends, for a good burger. We took this yearning as a good sign and started to make plans for getting her out of there. She was put into a full-body cast, which was the only way she could travel. We had to book nine seats together in the airplane so that they could bolt her across them. It was quite a trip.

The Liedermans met us at the airport along with the ambulance and we took her to Lenox Hill Hospital, where she was to be for another month. But at least she was home. She could start the long trip back to normalcy — or as close to normal as Alison has ever wanted to be.

Irish Stew

Serves 6

This is not the recipe for the oxtail soup that the taxi driver's wife served us on that memorable day. I thought about faking it but I didn't want to cheapen the memory. So, I'm substituting a recipe that I've cooked for decades. When you try it, you'll see that it has a similar effect: nurturing, warming, totally satisfying.

Irish stew is greater — far greater — than the sum of its parts. You throw together a few of the simplest, most pedestrian ingredients, get them simmering — not too violently, not too tamely — for a long time and out comes a miracle, a soothing, slightly spicy, totally satisfying experience. We used to have this in the old days when the weather was cold and we wanted to build some warmth from the inside, or we'd have it when show business turned our heads with its glitter and falseness and we needed to remind ourselves that simple is best. For that, there's nothing better than Irish stew.

There are a few important things to remember in making this recipe. First, make sure you use good water. If your local tap water contains a lot of chlorine or chemicals, it's worth going to the trouble and small expense of getting a few gallons of good spring water. It would be a shame to make this wonderful dish and have it come out smelling like a swimming pool. Second, use mutton rather than young lamb; the texture is better. Third, I would recommend you make more than you need for one meal, as this dish gets even better in the reheating.

3 pounds lamb (preferably mutton) cut from the leg, trimmed of as much fat and gristle as possible	3 pounds onions 3 pounds potatoes sea salt fresh ground pepper

Cut the lamb into 2-inch squares. Peel the onions and cut them into 2-inch chunks. Do the same with the potatoes. In a heavy-bottomed stockpot, put in a layer of the potatoes, then salt and pepper; then a layer of lamb chunks, salt, and pepper; then a layer of onions, salt, and pepper. Continue until everything's in. Then cover with your spring water just over the top of the last layer. Heat to a simmer and let it gently become stew — two to three hours should do. Serve in warm soup bowls with some crusty bread on the side to soak up whatever gravy you don't lap up with the potatoes.

Saint Martin

꙰ In my zealous, almost religious search for new sources of income to supplement my acting career, I finally managed to crack the inner circle of the voice-over fraternity. This is a small group of guys (and a smaller group of gals) whose voices you hear on radio and TV commercials. The jobs can range from the flat, businesslike "Member FDIC" tagged onto the end of a bank commercial to the voices of animals or even inanimate objects. A famous industry story tells of an actor who when auditioning for the voice of a pencil asked, "Do you see him as lead or mechanical?" I have been the voice of a dog, many parrots, and a pair of men's socks. It's a fun business. My access to this very profitable game was my Italian accent. It was known that I had dubbed Giannini and others, so every time there was a call for Italians, I would be submitted, and often as not I would get the job. I finally convinced the agent that I could speak in other dialects as well — including American — and after a while she got the point. The agency signed me and started to send me up on a regular basis.

My first big account — which means an ongoing job with one client — was Toys R Us. I was the voice of Geoffrey the Giraffe for two years. Just before Thanksgiving I would go into the studio for a full week, ten hours a day, and bang out hundreds of Christmas spots for Toys R Us. Geoffrey's voice was very high-pitched and benign so as not to frighten the children. To create this effect, I drained all the testosterone out of my voice and made him sound like a very tall, reticulated eunuch — a brilliant piece of character work; Stanislavsky would have been proud.

When I realized how much money this skinny gelding was going to bring in, I started to plan a romantic getaway with Jill. We hadn't sneaked off on our own since Max was born — actually, we had never taken a honeymoon of any kind — and we desperately needed it.

We sifted through brochures and put the word out to all our rich friends — where's the best, most exclusive, sexiest resort? With the best food of course. The consensus came back that a hotel called La Samanna on the French side of Saint Martin was the place we were looking for. Saint Martin was rightfully famous for its food. Like all islands, its provisions had to be brought in by boat or plane. But on the French side of Saint Martin, luxury provisions arrived via Air France from Paris daily. So items like poulet Bresse, fresh foie gras from Périgord, and real, unpasteurized, runny French cheeses, which were unobtainable in the States, were an everyday commodity in Saint Martin. And La Samanna, being the most exclusive resort on the island, also boasted the finest restaurant. We booked for five days, which was all Jill was willing to spend away from Max. The price was ridiculous, but it was all giraffe money, so what the hell.

Then the planning got under way, always nearly as much fun as the trip itself. We bought resort clothes — loose, silky things that were elegant and comfortable. I signed us up for sessions at a tanning parlor so we could hit the beaches with good color and a protective layer of store-bought tan. We bought books: Jill's covered the wildflowers native to the Caribbean; mine was called *A Guide to the World's Nude Beaches,* a very fine, informative, and surprisingly literate work — a real addition to my bookshelf.

We made plans for Max. We asked Veronica, who had been our nanny for more than a year, to move in for the week and bring her own kids along to keep Max company. This was a perfect situation; he would have playmates and we would get away guilt free. Sure we would. Veronica is Jamaican — now, don't get me wrong, we loved her, we trusted her, she made us laugh. But her breezy, laid-back, "don't worry, be happy" attitude made us nervous about going away. No matter how hard we tried, we couldn't get her tense enough. We walked her through some of the more dire possibilities that could come up during the week — kidnapping, fire, measles — and all she did was laugh.

"We be fine; you go have a good time."

We begged Alison, who was around fourteen and not into familial responsibilities, to help out, to keep an eye on things. "Yeah, right." No help there.

So off we went, our necks like steel rods, false smiles plastered on our faces, off we went to paradise. We flew in silence, Jill with her thoughts, me with mine — Jill trying desperately to quell her maternal instincts to hijack the plane and return to her baby; me, in complete denial, convincing myself that my feelings of anxiety, dislocation, and irritable-bowel syndrome were just a normal part of a fun getaway. We landed in a tropical downpour. The long drive from the airport to the other side of the island took forever on the rutted, rain-soaked dirt

road. It was then that Jill shared with me that she might have a
yeast infection.

We finally arrived, and La Samanna was indeed a beautiful
place. It sat like a Moorish castle, overlooking a perfect half-
moon beach, with indoor-outdoor tiled terraces kept cool by
the thick whitewashed walls and vaulted arches that led you
from one area to another. Everywhere were tropical flowers,
everywhere was a dazzling view, and at each photogenic little
bamboo table sat rich, perfect-looking people with real tans
who looked at us as if we had stumbled into the wrong place.

We checked in, I reconfirmed our dinner reservations, and
we went to our room. Jill immediately called home and, of
course, couldn't get a connection. In a panic she called the
desk. "I'm sorry, Mrs. Tucker, the lines are down for the moment. The storm. We'll call you as soon as we can get through."

We went down to the picturesque lobby to wait. I strolled
around to find a drugstore; we needed remedies for her infection and my stomach, which was getting worse by the minute.
There was no drugstore. We sat with our tropical rum drinks
and watched the storm pelt the coastline. My stomach rumbled
and lurched, competing with the thunder. The silver-haired
men with their young, sleek women sipped champagne and
sneered at us. Finally the man at the desk paged Jill; he had gotten through. I went with her and put my ear close to the phone.

"Hi, Veronica, how's it going?"

"It's fine," she sang.

"Is someone crying? Is that Max?"

"They're just playing, you know. He fell a little."

"Fell?"

"Just on the floor. Don't worry."

"Does he miss us?"

"No. He don't even know you're gone."

Dinner that night was a disaster. I couldn't get anything down. I felt bloated even though I hadn't eaten since we left New York. Tournedos in a shallot demi-glace reduction sat untouched on my plate; foie gras was returned to the kitchen — too rich. The wine was actually painful going down. Dessert was out of the question. I don't recall ever being so gastronomically depressed. It seemed like such a dreadful waste. And I managed to get a brown stain, shaped like the island of Anguilla, down the front of my new silk sports jacket. How could I get a stain without eating anything? The gods were laughing.

The storm subsided for a moment and we walked on the beach in the moonlight. We tried to be philosophical.

"I guess traveling isn't for us," said Jill, her thoughts far away.

"At least we know that now," said I. "At least this trip taught us that we shouldn't ever do this."

"God, I wish we were home," she said softly.

The sand managed to penetrate my socks. Little bugs bit my neck.

The next day we were rained out again. We drove over to the more commercial Dutch side of the island and shopped for things we didn't need. Then we gambled at a dreary little hotel casino, and lost. We drove back to La Samanna, read our books in silence, and etched another mark on the wall behind our bed. Only three days left.

But the next morning broke clear and sparkling and we woke to birds singing on our balcony. We had our breakfast out there looking at sailboats dotting the Caribbean. We watched the little yellow birds finish up the crumbs from my remarkably good croissant, obviously baked on the premises by someone with an authentic French accent. My stomach gave me signals that it was returning to its old, cast-iron self. I had another cup of rich, strong coffee, the kind you can never get in a hotel.

"I feel the itch to explore," I said, thumbing through the Caribbean section of my *Guide to the World's Nude Beaches.*

"Honey . . . ?"

Her eyes begged me to let her off the hook. She was backing out! After all those tanning sessions! I couldn't believe it.

"I'd feel self-conscious."

"It'll be a very freeing experience! You have to leap! Or your life will be over and you'll never have transcended your dreary little petty existence!" I was getting desperate.

"Well, I'll go, but I might keep my suit on."

"Jesus. You'll miss the whole experience." I tried to crush her with my disdain. "And besides, the sun'll be very good for your infection." The medical approach.

"I don't think it was a yeast infection. It's gone now."

This was very good news. I reached out and put my arm around her silky hips and pulled her toward me. This was the first time we had touched in two and a half days. It had been like dating a leper.

"We'll go and we'll see." I kissed her to let her know that no matter how many beautiful naked women were on the beach, she was the one I loved.

Nude beaches are not easy to get to. The guidebook led us to the end of a dirt road, which was miles off the main dirt road that led to the airport. This was a secondary dirt road that was so overgrown with weeds that you could barely see the dirt. We parked the car and after many false starts found the hidden trail that inched along the cliffs for miles before it slowly circled down through the rocks to a secluded beach below. I felt like Ponce de León.

"There was a perfectly beautiful beach at La Samanna that we could get to without killing ourselves," said the helpful wife. I chose not to answer; I was a man with a mission.

"And a lot of the girls there had their tops off."

I snorted derisively.

"La Samanna is a compound — a controlled environment. Nothing can happen there without the complete approval of the management."

"What do you think is going to happen? Are you expecting some kind of Roman orgy?"

I held my hand up to signal quiet and pointed below to the beach. We both stared in awe; we didn't breathe for what seemed minutes. For there below us on the pristine beach was a solitary woman — naked as a jay bird — sunning herself on the sand. Was she a mirage? Was my fantasy racing out of control from the heat and the danger of nearly falling off the cliff? Or was this the most beautiful, most voluptuous blond Euro-model that I have ever seen? Jill, of course, wanted to leave, something about not disturbing her privacy. But I was not to be denied. It was all I could do not to grab Jill's hand and leap us off the cliff like a pair of kamikaze Mexican cliff divers, but I controlled myself. We edged down to the beach.

We set out our blanket and towels about fifteen feet from her. Jill smiled at me indulgently — as if she had just gotten me a new puppy — as if to say, "This is what you've always wanted; I hope you're happy." And I was! I was jubilant. I leaped out of my shorts and felt the glorious freedom of being naked under the sun. I instantly started slathering suntan oil all over my body. When I got to the area heretofore least exposed, I was faced with a dilemma: how much time and attention should I give to oiling up this particular part? On the one hand, I didn't want to be accused of flagrant autoeroticism; on the other, it was the area I least wanted exposed to a bad sunburn. Was there an international protocol? As I pondered this, Jill calmly slipped out of her clothes and was applying her suntan oil. She gave me a huge Cheshire cat grin. An electric jolt shot through me; there we were — me and Jill and Heidi — with the beach and the sea to ourselves! I ran down to the sea and dove in — to cool my burgeoning enthusiasm — and Jill sauntered after me.

The Caribbean is like no other ocean. It's energizing and hospitable and gloriously buoyant. That's exactly how we felt — buoyant — as we dog-paddled in the sea and looked back at Greta's oil-soaked body pointing upward to the sun. Our energies floated to the surface of our skin, every pore opened and luxuriated in the feeling of freedom and excitement; the water seemed to be cooling us and heating us at the same time.

"Do you think they're real?" asked Jill of Solange's remarkable breasts.

"Definitely."

"They point straight up."

Indeed her whole body was flabbergasting — and perfectly still. She hadn't moved since we got there. A doubt cast its shadow on my perfect day; was she real? Maybe the ministry of tourism placed these perfect, plastic, oil-bronzed Euro-models all over the hard-to-get-to beaches in order to raise tourist morale and increase the sale of suntan oil. But just then she stirred; she rose up like Botticelli's Venus on the half shell, reapplied her oil, and turned over, revealing just as impressive a backside as front.

The three of us spent another hour together, sunning, swimming, reading our books, and just generally being nude. Ingrid never spoke to us, or even glanced at us as far as I could tell. Finally she pulled on some shorts and a halter, gathered her things, and climbed back up the cliff to return to the world of clothes, leaving Jill and me alone in our own private Eden. The three of us had spent such a short time together, and yet we felt we knew her. Some people are like that.

We explored the beach and found a little cave that gave us a chance to get out of the sun. We poked around the tide pools and chased tiny sand crabs that tried to escape by burying themselves in the wet sand. We swam in the incredibly clear blue water, diving under and exploring the white, sandy bottom with the little yellow and green fish that lived in the neighborhood. We dried off in the warm breeze. I had won a convert to the world of bare-assed hedonism.

"It feels good, no?"

"It has its moments," she said, and blushed from stem to stern.

We drove back to the hotel to shower. We found sand in places that God never intended it to be. Our bodies were warm from the sun and the salt and the exposure in general. We rubbed moisturizer on each other. And one thing led to another. And another. And then we were hungry.

It was after three and the hotel had finished serving lunch; once again, no meal at La Samanna. We got in the car and explored the coast between Marigot and Grand Case, the two largest towns on the French side of the island. We stumbled onto a little roadhouse right on the beach that had a sign that said Open. It looked like a permanent sign. We were the only customers, and it turned out to be much more than it first seemed. It was actually a tiny guest house with a couple of ocean-front rooms for rent connected to a restaurant of small proportions but no small ambition. It was the dream of a young French couple who had moved to the island a few years before — a place that combined fresh, exciting food and very personal attention with the laid-back atmosphere of the Caribbean. They were delighted to see us. At their place, lunch was served any time you were hungry.

A great meal can happen for many different reasons. The food, obviously, the ambiance, the company, the hospitality of the host. But I think the most crucial component is receptivity — just being in the mood to receive pleasure. And I don't think I can recall another moment in my life when my receptors were glowing with more intensity than they were that afternoon in Saint Martin. We ordered simply — local lobsters, salad, and a bottle of very good Chablis. We held hands across the table and I watched Jill's eyes catch the afternoon light. They were incredibly blue — like in those TV commercials where everything else is in black-and-white and one item is lit up in blazing color. They were that blue. And only the day before they had been a kind of gray. Now, we all know that her eyes didn't change; it was me — my perception of her — my receptivity to her. And it was the same with the food. What could have been ordinary, or just good, was sublime. We couldn't get enough. It wasn't until the lobsters came that we realized how hungry we were — it must have been all that doggy-paddling. The lobsters had simply been fished out of the water, split, brushed with butter, and grilled over a wood fire. The shells were charred black in spots and the meat was perfect — sweet and smoky. It didn't need any melted butter, but there it was on the table, so what the hell. One big, chunky, buttery mouthful after another. We weren't in the mood to deny ourselves anything. Our bodies seemed to gobble up every overindulgence we offered up. We ordered a third lobster to share, although we both knew it wouldn't be an even split. Our hosts brought out a large wooden salad bowl filled with lettuces from their own garden in a tart, faintly mustardy vinaigrette and placed it between us to share. They had caught on to the orgiastic spirit of the meal and seemed to be enjoying it as much as we were. We couldn't get enough of it, or of the cool, rich wine, or of each other. We breathed in, our faces almost touching, to catch a whiff of each other's contentment. You know that smell that's in the air when bread is just becoming itself in the oven? There was something of that in the air between us. Roasted serenity. Some people just know how to travel, I guess.

SIXTEEN

L.A. — Law and Otherwise

꙾ It all started at dinner with the Bochcos. They were in New York for a few days on their way to London and asked us to join them at the Four Seasons. They were on top of the world at that moment and wanted to show us what life was like from up there. *Hill Street Blues,* which was Steven's creation, had just finished its fourth year and was heralded by everyone as one of the finest shows in television history. It had just captured a record number of Emmy nominations — one of which was for Barbara's work as best supporting actress — and was now being released in all the foreign markets. Hence the trip to London. They would give interviews, be wined and dined by all the foreign network execs, be recognized by cabbies in the streets of London, and just generally bask in the intense glow of worldwide recognition. This was a business trip that would be pure pleasure.

They were already into the second basket of rolls when we showed up. As we approached the table, they stood up to embrace us, and I noticed that Stevie had that shy, almost rueful grin that he gets on his face when he's conquered the world against all odds and everyone's predictions. The smile says, "I know I should be self-effacing and modest at a moment like this, but fuck it, I did it and you didn't." It's one of my favorite looks. We sat and ordered drinks, told all the latest jokes, and took in the surroundings.

The Four Seasons is one of my favorite places to have dinner — whether I'm with internationally famous people or not. The room is spacious and elegant and has those shimmering curtains that seem to be made of spun gold. There are many levels to the room, so that the waiters and captains always seem to be walking up or down curved stairways to get to you. This restaurant exudes its own power, and when I'm there it makes me feel powerful too. It inevitably moves me to order a more expensive wine than I can really afford. Which is probably how they pay for cleaning all those gold curtains. Anyway, this dinner was on the Bochcos, which was good because Jill and I were in one of our "theater cycles" and not in the chips.

We babbled on about old times and new times and how the Bochcos and the Tuckers were destined always to be on opposite coasts and wasn't that a shame, when Stevie slyly slipped a hand grenade into the conversation.

"We just wrote an episode — a two-parter, actually — where this couple from the Midwest comes to L.A. for a vacation and everything conceivable happens to them. It's one of our funniest scripts and it just occurred to me while we were sitting here that you guys could do it."

He turned to Barbara and she nodded enthusiastically, "They'd be perfect."

Now, let me say right here that I don't think this idea "just occurred" to him over his rack of lamb at the Four Seasons. Nothing "just occurs" to Stevie. He's like one of those Russian chess masters who's at least seven moves ahead of you at all times.

Jill and I looked at each other, she thinking about whether she wanted to do television, me thinking about next month's rent, both of us wondering whether working together would be good or disastrous for our relationship. Most acting couples avoid it like the plague.

"Now, we can't fly you out or give you expenses or anything. We don't do that for guest stars; but if you could make your own way out there, I think we would all have a great time."

So, he was negotiating the contract already. No expenses, no flight.

"How much would we . . ."

"We'll give you top of the show."

This turned out to be about twenty-five hundred dollars apiece, which was a lot of money for us in those days, and my head was still buzzing with the phrase "guest stars." I liked that. So, we all shook hands and said we'd see them in L.A. when they got back from London.

If we were going to do this on the cheap, we had to find a good place to stay. The Bochcos asked us to move in with them — and this was a tempting offer. They were living in a beautiful house in Santa Monica in those days and we would be quite comfortable. But after thinking about it, we decided that it might get a little too incestuous. What if Jill and I weren't any good and *Hill Street* had to let us go? What if they had to replace us with Frank and Kathie Lee? It might make life around the breakfast table a little tense. So we called Judith and Rene Auberjonois and asked them if we could rent the little guest house above their garage. They said we could have it for nothing, which is what we hoped they would say, and the problem was solved.

Hill Street was shot at CBS-Radford Studios in Studio City. After settling in at the Auberjonoises', we drove over there in our little rental car to meet everybody. We impressed ourselves when we dropped our name to the studio guard and he actually opened the gate. He directed us to Bochco's office. Marilyn, the ever faithful secretary, organizer, and guard dog, who had been with Steven for years, ushered us right into the middle of a story meeting. He ended the meeting, cleared the office, and had us sit down. I wondered then whether he knew how important he was making us feel. I know now that of course he did.

He personally ushered us around the offices. We met the director and the other writers who were all hard at work on "our" scripts. Then he took us over to wardrobe, where we were measured and fitted and showed our costumes. Our excitement was hard to contain. We were the guest stars and we were being treated as such. We even had our own trailers with our name on the door. Never mind that they were small and dingy and had chemical toilets that were dysfunctional; never mind that an illegal migrant worker wouldn't have been caught dead in one of these trailers; they were our own personal "star wagons" and we thought they were pretty grand.

Shooting started a couple of days later and went very well from the outset. After the first day, Jill and I felt as if we had just knocked off a bank and gotten away with it. This was fun! It was ten times easier than acting with a stranger. All we had to do was look at each other and all sorts of buttons got pushed automatically. And because we were doing comedy, there was that extra-special feeling of harmony or trust. It was as if a third entity existed between us — the joke — and if we trusted each other's timing completely, we could make it happen. We used to say it was like being blindfolded trapeze artists; we just believed that the other would be there with the right timing and the right energy to complete the catch. It was amazing to hurtle through space with your eyes closed knowing that your mate would be there to pull you through. Not only was this great fun professionally, but we kicked our marriage up a few notches at the same time. There's nothing like knowing you can trust that other person and that she can do your job at least as well as you can.

The show was classic *Hill Street*. We played a naive couple who were mugged, had their car stolen, had their suitcases stolen, and got roughed up all within minutes of arriving in L.A. for a vacation. Then the treatment they received from the police was even worse than they had gotten from the muggers. The final scene was a lineup where Jill's character had to identify her stolen dress, which was being worn by a six-foot-tall transvestite. It was pure Bochco, and we had the feeling that Stevie was very pleased with the way it all worked out.

When we got back to New York, life was different somehow; I had bitten the apple; that little snake known as network TV had wormed its way into my consciousness, and I would never again be that innocent, pure artist untainted by crass commercialism. Even Jill was affected. She went on and on about how she didn't want to do a TV series, which made me sit up and take notice because no one had yet asked her to do a TV series. That little snake had given her a good bite too. The seeds, planted by Bochco, of L.A. and TV and our working together were now germinating in the backs of our minds. They would lie dormant for another year or so as we went on with our New York careers, but things were definitely stirring back there.

This Bochco-L.A. connection goes back a long way in my history — more than thirty years. Which is odd when you consider that Steven is even less from L.A. than I am. He's pure New York — Eighty-third Street on the West Side. But every time I've gone out to the West Coast, Stevie has been either the instigator of the trip or somehow in the center of it.

I first laid eyes on him in 1962 at the student union snack bar at Carnegie Tech in Pittsburgh. He was the center of attention at a table of disreputable looking Dramats, which is what they patronizingly called the drama majors at this institution primarily dedicated to turning out engineers. Anyway, he was holding forth at this particularly arty-looking table. He had long hair and olive-colored skin and that nasal New York superior sneer in his voice. He was wearing torn jeans and a shiny Puerto Rican–looking shirt. He was everything my middle-class upbringing told me to stay away from. This was the very "element" I knew I must avoid. I was in chinos; I had on a blue shirt with a button-down collar; I had Bass Weejuns on my feet. I was a real college man. Just because I was aspiring to be an actor was no reason for me to give up my middle-class values.

Because of my superior moral fiber and keen sense of integrity, it took a full two weeks before I gave up all those values and plunged headlong into the bohemian world of the drama department. I think I sold the Weejuns to a sophomore chemical engineer who wore a slide rule connected to his belt in a quick-draw holster. They looked much more at home on him.

But I still avoided Bochco. And he and the rest of the "artsy" table took little interest in me. Although I had become an artist and let my hair grow long and curly and stopped trying to straighten it like a gentile's, friendship with these New Yorkers still seemed too dangerous a step to take.

The icebreaker was touch football. When the weekend came and our intense drama-school schedule ground to a halt, we found ourselves just a group of eighteen- or nineteen-year-old boys who hadn't had a chance to meet most of the girls yet and who had a lot of excess energy to burn. It was autumn, the season when a young man's fingers twitch to get around a football. What started as a catch between two or three of us quickly grew into a pickup game. We moved over to one of the athletic fields, chose sides, and started to play in earnest. Almost immediately the cliques and hierarchies began to reshuffle. Now it didn't matter where you came from or what you looked like or how much you knew about Grotovsky. The only thing that mattered was whether you could throw or block or fake the other guy out of his shoes. By the time the game was over and we strolled over to Skibo for coffee, I was at Bochco's table — never to leave.

He told a story that day — replete with Jewish accent — about an octogenarian who married an eighteen-year-old bride.

"Mine darlink, I'm going to ravage you and pillage and make you scream," he says to the young girl before making love.

"Mine darlink, the next time I'm going to ravage you and pillage you, I'm also goink to make you sweat."

"Why sweat?" asks the young girl.

"Because the next time I ravage and pillage you," says the exhausted old man, "It vill be August."

The table cracked up. There must have been eight or ten of us football players — some of whom had never heard a Jewish joke told properly, with the right dialect, inflection, and facial gestures. But I was in my element. I had sat at the feet of the master — my Uncle Benny — who regaled us from his Barcalounger every Saturday night with the finest Jewish humor. I told the story of the same octogenarian who goes to buy his first custom-made suit. This is an elaborate joke with many characters, each with his own set of gestures. It is the classic shaggy-Jew joke. When I finished, there wasn't a dry seat in the house. The whole table was aching with laughter. Then

Bochco weighed in with the one about the old Jewish man at the proctologist, which cannot be related on these pages for obvious reasons. That reminded me about the old Jewish man who has only eight hours to live. When he tells his wife the sad news, she offers to make him a wonderful dinner for his last night on earth. He replies that he would rather stay up all night making love. "Easy for you," she says, "you don't have to get up in the morning." One joke led to another; it wasn't a competition, it was a celebration, a cultural homecoming.

Lord, he was funny. And strangely shy and vulnerable. His humor grew out of his shyness; he used it like a shield to deflect people. He also used it like a dagger. He would say the very things that everyone was thinking but wouldn't dare say. He turned unutterable truth into shocking humor that had the effect of ridding the room of all hypocrisy in one clean stroke. I had never met anyone like him.

Maybe the humor is what's held us together all these years. That and what we use the humor to cover. We tell each other jokes; one leads to another and we chortle away, not caring that we've heard them before — that almost makes it better. We used to say that when we get old, we'll sit on a park bench, feed the pigeons, and tell stories to each other in thick Jewish accents. It's our opinion that these accents come to one later in life, no matter where you grew up.

The bond between us strengthened when I acted in his play. This happened during our sophomore year. He had written a one-acter, which was required as part of the curriculum for playwriting majors. It was about a woman and two men. One of the men wore black and the other white. It was a symbolic kind of thing. They represented the two sides of man's nature in relation to woman. Okay, it was a student play, but hell, he was a student. Guess which one of the men I played? Right, the good one. Even then. I thought it was a very nice play, but Steven completely denies paternity these days. When I bring it up, he nervously drifts over to his giant collection of Emmy Awards and tries to hide behind them. But he did write that play. I was there. What I remember most about the experience was that during rehearsals the budding playwright kept saying that he was only doing this as a course requirement, that it was a pretentious piece of drivel, and that he was going to Hollywood as soon as possible to become a big mogul. Even then.

Our friendship really bloomed around that time. Not only did we make each other laugh, but we could tell each other our secrets — what we *really* thought and aspired to. We shared our dreams. And this kind of intimacy was rare in drama school, which was a cynical place. And it was especially rare among men. But Stevie and I felt safe with one another.

He got married during our junior year to Gaby Levin. And I was their adopted son. I think mostly they had me around so they wouldn't have to be alone with each other. At least when I was there, we always had something to laugh about. Gaby would cook dinner for us. They had me over every night.

"What are we having?"

"Chicken," Gaby would say.

"Chicken how?"

"Chicken. You put it in the oven until it gets brown."

It was a good thing the meals were free.

True to his word, Steven got himself a job in the mailroom at Universal Studios — a perfect starting place for the budding mogul. So right after graduation he and Gaby were heading West, and they asked me to come with them. I had a job at the Long Wharf Theater in New Haven coming up in the fall, but I figured I could test the waters in Los Angeles over the summer and see what I thought of it.

Gaby had flown out to get them settled, and Stevie and I drove across the country in his '65 Mustang. Talk about a bonding experience. We did nothing but talk the whole way across the country. But there was a rift or a tension inherent in the situation. Stevie was driving headlong toward his future, and I felt I was driving away from mine. His destiny was in Hollywood and the West, and all my training and aspirations were for the theater and the East. And he was so much clearer in terms of his goals. His vision of success had a laserlike clarity — wealth, power, fame — which is exactly what came about as the years passed. My vision, on the other hand, was muddled. I don't think I could have told you then what I wanted out of my life. There was the art thing; there was the money thing; there was the success thing; and there was the fear of success thing — I was a mess.

And so the drive across the country allowed us to get to know each other intimately on the one hand, and to realize the vastness of our differences on the other. By the time we reached Los Angeles, we agreed that our lives were heading in opposite directions. Stevie went off to climb the ladder of success and I walked around the hot streets of L.A. wondering what I was doing there. I lived with the Bochcos in their tiny apartment and watched their marriage start to go sour. Then I moved into a very nice broom closet right off the Sunset Strip, where I had to fold up my sofa bed if I wanted to open the refrigerator. After a few weeks of that, I flew back east to start my long journey through the repertory theaters of America.

Stevie and I wrote letters. I wish I still had them, because we would laugh over them today. They were about values and belief systems and a lot of twenty-one-year-old crap like that. I criticized him, and he me. We went our different ways but always stayed in touch.

Now here we were twenty years later. He had realized every dream and more. I was turning forty and having to face the fact that many of my grandest dreams might never come true. But Stevie felt otherwise. As I said, he was always at least seven moves ahead. From the *Hill Street* experience, he sensed something in the chemistry between Jill and me that he felt should be mined a bit deeper. Unbeknownst to us, he went to MTM and told them to try to develop something for us. But his relationship with the executives there was nearing its end and they weren't interested in his advice. So when he went over to Twentieth Century Fox to begin his tenure there, he took the idea with him. Which brings us to our next significant dinner — again in New York, this time at the Palm.

Steven called us — this was now about a year and a half after our *Hill Street* segments — and told us that he and Barbara were coming into town and wanted to take us to dinner. He said he had a favor he wanted to ask us. It turned out that Jill was out of town doing a movie, so I met them in the lobby of the Plaza and we went on to dinner from there. When he came off the elevator and first laid eyes on me, he started to laugh.

"What?"

"You've put on a few."

This was true; I had gained about eight to ten pounds in the year or so since I had seen him. There seems to be something about turning forty that keeps the weight on you like nothing else — except possibly turning fifty.

"It's okay. It's not exactly what we had in mind, but okay."

When I asked him what he was talking about, he waved me off and said we would get to it at dinner.

Now, the Palm is one of those restaurants that has my number. It gives large portions and I take them. Along with my steak that could easily have fed four people, I had a huge platter of hash brown potatoes in front of me and a platter of onion rings. Bochco was witnessing firsthand how I had gained all those pounds. He was having fish — no fat, either on the fish or on him. As far as I can see, he hasn't gained an ounce since college. Like I said, we went different ways.

"So what favor do you want to ask me," I said as the cheese-cake came. For me, not him.

"I'm writing a new show, a law show, and I want to pattern two of the characters after you and Jill."

I immediately put down my fork with the cheesecake on it. I knew that television puts ten pounds on you, so that makes twenty before I even got started.

"The characters will court and fall in love and eventually they may marry. We haven't gotten that far yet."

"I don't know for sure if Jill will do a TV series. She says she won't, but this could be different."

"We'll worry about that when we get there. Right now I just want your okay to write these characters with you in mind. It'll help me get them onto the page."

So I gave him permission, which was big of me. But he had paid for dinner, so I owed him one. That night I talked to Jill on the phone and told her all about it. I didn't let on how excited I was, because I knew she didn't want to move to L.A. She is a nester and her kids were in good schools. She didn't want to change anything. I, on the other hand, was already composing my acceptance speech for the Emmies.

About three months later a script arrived. It was tentatively titled *L.A. Law.* We thought they would have to change that. Jill got to it before I did, and I watched from the other room as she inhaled the character of Ann Kelsey. Before she finished her first reading, she was saying the lines under her breath. She was already learning them. It was clear she wasn't going to let any other actress near this role. We were going to California.

About two weeks before we flew out to film the pilot, we were having dinner with Steven and Faye Collins. We told them about how excited we were about the script and the possible move west. They had both done series, so they knew the ropes.

"You remember that blue MG I have out there?" asked Steve.

Well, of course I remembered it. It was the same color as my Sunbeam Alpine from twenty-five years before and much better looking. It was a robin's egg blue MGA, which, after the XK 140 Jag and the Austin Healy, is one of the classic sports car designs of all time.

"I'm selling it," says Steve.

"I'm buying it," says Mike. And the deal was consummated on the spot.

Jill gave me that "You are Mr. Toad" look, but I didn't care. I had just bought the perfect California car for the budding TV star. I could buzz around the freeways waving to starlets, being careful not to let my white silk scarf catch in the wire wheels. I could work on my tan. Never mind that we weren't moving to L.A. until we found out whether the show was a hit or not. Never mind that we couldn't afford to buy a car. "Putt-Putt," said Mr. Toad, his eyes as big as saucers.

Mike and Jill, Max and Alison fly out — first class to L.A. It's midwinter, so we have that extra excitement of leaving the slush and grime of New York for the sun-drenched paradise of California. We'll only be staying for three weeks to shoot the pilot; then we'll come back to New York until July, get our lives in order, then return to finish shooting the rest of the first season.

We're met at the airport by Bochco. He has his huge Mercedes so that we can fit all the luggage inside. He seems as excited as we are. He's beaming. He insists on carrying all the bags himself. It occurs to me that this is the culmination of a dream — not only for me, but for Steven as well. Each of us from his own perspective is fulfilling the fantasy that we talked about twenty-five years earlier when we drove across the country in his Mustang. But all these thoughts are in the back of my mind. Foremost, I'm thinking about my robin's egg blue MG, which is being stored at a mechanic's shop in Studio City, twenty miles out of our way.

"I need one more favor, Stevie," I say as he's hoisting three hundred pounds of luggage into his trunk. "Can you drive me out to get my car?"

Never mind that the most important man in television has taken a day off from his very busy schedule to be my skycap for the day. Never mind that my wife and children would like to get settled in our hotel after a long trip — I want my sports car. We compromise. First we'll drive Jill and the kids to the hotel and unload the luggage, then Stevie will drive me out to Studio City to get my car. After that, I'll follow him back — because I have no idea how to get around in this crazy town — and we'll meet everyone for dinner at the Ivy at the Shore. A perfect plan.

The minute I start the engine of the MG — it has one of those pull starters on the dashboard, very cool — it starts to rain. As we know, this is my fate in life. The mechanic, Steven, and I wrestle the convertible top up — of course, it leaks — and we're on our way. I'm trying to follow Stevie, but the windshield wipers are not terribly effective. This is a car that's meant to be driven in the sunshine with the top down. Steven senses my difficulty and slows down. The two of us create a strange picture, driving in close tandem on the Ventura Freeway at thirty-five miles an hour. When we finally get to Ocean Avenue in Santa Monica — only blocks from our destination —

Steven stops for a red light and I plow the MG headlong into the rear end of his four-million-dollar Mercedes. There is a long pause as I peer past the faulty windshield wipers to see his reaction. Is he furious? Is he on the car phone calling to recast the role of Stuart Markowitz? The fog on the window clears a little and I see him turned to me, looking back through his rear window. And he's laughing. He's laughing his ass off. And I start to laugh — a little from relief, I'm sure — but mostly from love. How can I explain this? For twenty-five years we made each other laugh. It was our thing. We shared a view of life that nothing was too serious, too reverential not to get a laugh out of somehow. At times the laugh might be a dark one, but it was always there. And this absurd moment on the streets of Santa Monica, in the rain, was a culmination, an affirmation, of that bond between us.

Two months later that philosophy was put to a severe test. I was standing in the waiting room of a hospital in New York, waiting for Jill to come out of the operating room. I called Steven at his office in L.A.

"Jill has cancer."

And as I stood there, talking on the pay phone, hyperventilating and crying, he slowly took me out of my despair and into the future.

"We'll make a special schedule. No one will have to know why. We'll work around her radiation treatments. This is no death sentence, Micky. This is not the way she's going to die."

And right there he went to work. He called Barbara Kadell, who is one of the heads of the radiology department at UCLA. She set up Jill's radiation treatments. Meanwhile, Bochco personally guaranteed Jill's insurance situation, without which the studio would not hire her to do the series. Within two weeks of the operation, we moved to L.A. to begin shooting. We were reeling. We were facing mortality on a very basic level at the same time that we were about to become immortal in the eyes of the public. I remember an interview we gave about halfway into that season, just shortly after the "Venus Butterfly" episode went on the air. We were very much the flavor of the month at that moment and the interviewer asked us how we handled this sudden rush of fame. What we didn't tell her was that success and fame were not on our minds these days. We were thinking more about survival and about holding on to each other as tightly as we could. We had a secret, and no one knew but us. And Bochco.

Just this year Barbara and Steven were up in Big Sur with us. I hauled Steven up a huge hill, which has, at the top, the most beautiful view I have ever seen. You look north to the Point Sur lighthouse and beyond to Carmel; south is the classic Big Sur view — mountains falling gracefully to the sea. The crashing surf was below us, the mountains to our backs, and we sat on a little park bench, put there by a thoughtful park ranger, and talked like old Jewish men — just like we said we would. We talked about our past, as we always do. And a little about the future. We talked about our growing appreciation of silence, about the need to be still and listen to ourselves. We talked about our friendship. And then we told the one about the two Jewish women in the lavatory, talking about their sons. . . . And we laughed until tears came to our eyes; we laughed as though we had never heard it before.

Paris

❦

There are few better feelings in the world than coming out of a chilly evening into the warm, bustling atmosphere of a Paris bistro. The instant you walk through the door, your cold cheeks are heated by the aromatic blast of roasting meats and sautéing garlic and the commingling buzz of waiters, diners, and cooks. Such was our entrance into L'Ami Louis early in May, where we went to celebrate our twentieth wedding anniversary. There was sawdust on the floor, decades of grease on the walls and ceilings, and an excitement that fairly vibrated up from the soles of our feet. Not that phony kind of excitement that modern restaurants try to manufacture by lining the floors and ceilings with concrete so as to reverberate the room's desperation from one hard surface to another, but real excitement made up of the diners' hungry anticipation, the waiters' sassy insouciance, the popping of corks, and the sizzle of snails in garlic and butter.

I had heard about L'Ami Louis for years. Everyone who knew me and my penchant for good eating told me that this was the place for me. And so it is. It caters to my particular eating disorder — oculosis grandiosis — or, in the vernacular, having eyes larger than one's stomach. Now, I must point out that this malady only exists if the food is delectable — not too precious, not overly fussy, not too subtle (sorry, gastronomes), but satisfying in the deepest, most sensuous, satyr-pleasing way; when you approach that thin line between food and sex, and then erase the line, that's the kind of food I'm talking about.

We started with fois gras. It was brought to the table with a loaf of French bread, crusty and still warm so that we could spread the silky goose liver onto it and into it. They brought each of us a portion that consisted of three bricks of fois gras — bricks the size they build apartment houses with. There was no way that we could eat all of it without having a major coronary occlusion on the spot. But, as always, if the food is good enough, I can find room. The fois gras disappeared, brick by brick; more hot bread was placed on the table to help convey the liver to its final resting place. I not only finished mine but helped Jill clean her plate as well.

It was right about then that the wine thing came up. We had been avoiding it for the last couple of weeks, but it was sitting there between us like a large polka-dot elephant that neither of us wanted to look at. But now the fois gras was screaming for a great Bordeaux to help wash it down and there was no way of avoiding it any longer.

I had been off the sauce for a while, giving my kidneys and Jill's nervous system a well-deserved vacation. But the thought of coming to Paris — especially to L'Ami Louis — and not drinking wine seemed insane to me, so I brought up these thoughts to Jill a few weeks before our departure. She was understandably nervous. She worried that a little wine would lead to a lot of wine and that our honeymoon would suffer the consequences. I told her that if she was concerned, I wouldn't do it — after all, I certainly didn't want any kind of tension between us. Then she relented and said that if I wanted to have a little wine with some incredible meal, she would join me and not be tense about it.

"I think tonight's the night," I said casually as I spread some more fois gras.

Thud. The silence was impressive. I wasn't able to look directly into her eyes, which was a tip-off that I was as nervous as she was.

I called the waiter over and ordered half a bottle of Château la Mission Haut Brion. If I was going off the wagon, I wanted to go in style. Jill gave me that look that Jane Wyman gave to Ray Milland in *The Lost Weekend*.

"If it really bothers you, I won't do it. It's not worth screwing up our vacation."

"No. It's all right. Really."

And she gave me a weak smile letting me know that it wasn't all right one bit.

"Besides, red wine has all these antioxidants that prevent heart attacks, so there's even a chance it could help me live through this meal."

That did it. The waiter poured the wine and we each had a taste. It was seriously good. I knew I had made the right choice. Because of the layoff, I felt a buzz immediately. My skin warmed, my taste buds jumped up and down like little kids let out for recess, my arteries opened, and I spread another piece of bread with a large slather of liver. The evening was proceeding apace. But it was tainted now. Pandora's box had been reopened, and we all know how unpredictable that bitch can be.

The next course was chicken. Now, when I say chicken, you must understand that we're talking about an entirely different animal from what we get here in the States. The chickens over there actually have a taste of their own — a rich, powerful taste that leaps into your mouth and announces, "Hello, I am your chicken." The birds we have become accustomed to in America — even those called free-range chickens — are, alas, essentially tasteless. The better ones have a nice texture, maybe a hint of taste, but mostly they are there to convey the essence of whatever sauce or marinade is on them. We have grown used to chicken as a neutral taste.

What an amazing surprise to bite into the whole roast chicken that was delivered to each of us at L'Ami Louis. Yes, that's right, a whole three-and-a-half-pound chicken — each. And the crispy brown skin had been liberally basted with something that I had never tasted before. It was very rich, darkly aromatic, faintly gamy — everything I love — and it suffused the crackly skin with a taste that complemented the flesh of the chicken perfectly. What was it?

It was goose fat, my friends. Everything at L'Ami Louis was liberally bathed in goose fat. The chickens, their incredibly tasty leg of lamb, the huge platter of garlic potatoes that now sat glistening at the center of our table, all had been pan roasted in butter and, yes, goose fat. Goose fat coated everything, the green beans, the walls, the waiters, everything. This was a new sin for me. And I submerged myself in it like a man on a desert island who suddenly discovers a boatful of Dallas cheerleaders.

The evening was starting to feel out of control; the wine, the remnants of jet lag, the unusually high content of animal fat in my arteries, all mingled together in my head to create a sense of unreality. I gazed across the table at Jill; she looked back at me with a look of concern. Had I finally indulged myself past the point that even I could rationalize? I reached out to touch her hand, to regain a sense of reality, and as our hands touched, I lost my mind. It was terrifying. I actually imagined that I heard an eerily beautiful woman's voice singing the first few bars of "Stormy Weather." I panicked. The goose fat had congealed inside my brain, or the wine had loosened a screw, but for some reason the CD player inside my head was playing "Stormy Weather" and I had no control over it.

"Don't know why, there's no sun up in the sky . . ."

What brought me back to earth was the slow realization that I wasn't the only one hearing the song. The other customers were, one by one, slowing their chewing and cocking an ear to listen. The waiters skipped a beat in their serving rhythm, and I noticed as ours passed by that he looked at me and raised his eyes to heaven, as if to say, "Here we go again." Even the cooks stopped their cacophony to listen.

At the table behind us and to my left, a woman — indeed a young and rather beautiful woman — had decided for some reason to stand up by her chair and sing "Stormy Weather." No one knew why. Perhaps not even she. It's possible that her table had had a much larger dose of antioxidants than we had, because they seemed to be feeling no pain. The amazing thing was how good she was. This was no drunken rendition to be laughed at or hooted down; it was good — really good. Slowly the room stopped all activity and just listened to her. And when she was done there was a long pause and then a thunderous ovation. She sat down and plunged right back into her goose fat.

We were all delighted! It was like being there the night that Hank Aaron hit the home run, or when that mafioso got gunned down outside of Sparks Steak House in New York. We were witnesses to history. Unexpected observers to an event that would be talked about for years to come. The restaurant's energy kicked up a point or two. Everyone felt that this was a special night.

A few minutes later a blonde from another table — after some encouragement from her drunken companions — stood up to sing her song. We knew this must be a mistake. The first song was magic. The second must suffer in comparison. But no. This singer too was very good. She belted out that song from *Evita* with a big, professional voice. She had total confidence in herself and her voice and we were dazzled — yet again. The restaurant went berserk — shouting, banging spoons on glasses, standing ovations. The chefs were banging soup ladles on giant pots in the back to offer their support.

The women hugged each other. Had they ever met before? Were they French or American? We didn't know. Only that they were good-looking and very talented, a bit loaded and not at all inclined to stop. Next there was a duet. "Summertime." They lowered their voices and the room went silent. No one breathed as we listened to the two voices find harmonies and blend into the haunting Gershwin melody. Now we were all friends; we were related; we were there on the night when magic happened. Whenever Paris is mentioned, we will tell the story of this night — each in his or her own way. My rendition will feature goose fat, because that's the way I am.

We did everything we were supposed to do in Paris that trip. We saw Jill's obligatory museums and we ate at my obligatory restaurants, we took the snapshots and wrote the postcards. We did all the "shoulds." But the best day we had   one of the best days we've ever had — was when we did nothing.

Paris is a sly old whore. And you won't find her if you go chasing after her. But if you sit back and wait and have the sense to make a day or two with no plans — none at all — then she'll roll over for you. If you're in no hurry, she'll show you some old tricks; she'll lie back and smile and open her thighs like the ancient courtesan she is. And with the supreme confidence of an old pro, she'll titillate you and teach you and pick your pockets clean without ever giving you a moment of regret.

We woke up late and ordered breakfast in our room. We were staying at the Ritz in a beautiful suite overlooking the courtyard below, where in good weather, lunch was served al fresco. Room service at the Ritz is an indulgence. From Jill's fifty-dollar bowl of oatmeal (it was good) to my coffee and croissants (the best ever — in all the world) to the starched creases in the heavy linen tablecloth and the heft of the old silverware, this was a class operation.

We dressed in jeans and sneakers and set out for the Marais, an old section of Paris that's been reclaimed — much like Soho in New York — by young, stylish Parisians, with shops and restaurants and galleries. We had discovered it a few days before when we went to the Picasso Museum, which is housed in an old *hôtel,* or townhouse, in the Marais. Today we would just browse. We came across a gallery that was showing Matisse drawings — pen and ink drawings, framed simply — for about fifty thousand dollars apiece. I immediately started figuring out how to rationalize the purchase. "We're doing the show for another year, which is just found money really, and it'll be a wonderful investment, and Matisse is really my favorite when all is said and done — well, one of my favorites. . . ." The only thing that stopped me was that the drawings weren't particularly interesting — which is why they were being sold for only fifty thousand. A good one would bring millions. But we had fun dreaming of an original Matisse on the wall of our bedroom before we moved on down the street.

We found a used-clothing store on a street filled with interesting boutiques and cafés. Jill wanted to try on some things. After all, old clothes from Paris are a lot more interesting than old clothes from L.A. There was a rack of coats — sort of like peacoats — that were either Navy surplus or old gendarmes' coats from the 1930s. They were black, about hip length, with big black buttons that came right up to the collar. We found one that fit Jill perfectly. She put it on and buttoned it up to the top and turned the collar up so that her face was just peeking out under her bangs. It made her smile. She ran around the store looking at herself in all the different mirrors, giggling as she went. There was something about this coat that tickled her. And me too. She looked about fourteen — her face flushed with fun, she was a combination of Leslie Caron and Julie Christie. Not a bad combination. I had to have her immediately.

"Taxi," I called out the doorway of the store, paying quickly for the coat.

"No, don't wrap it; she'll wear it home."

We sped back to the Ritz. Lunch service was just starting in the courtyard below our window and we were torn as to which appetite we needed to satisfy more directly. We figured lunch we could always get.

I talked her into leaving the coat on. Just the coat. If she had had a pair of Mary Janes with those little white socks . . . ah, well. We approached that line again — the one between food and sex — and erased it again. Now we were seriously hungry. We hurried over to the Île de la Cité to a bistro we knew that sat beside a little park. The food was simple and hot and perfect. Leek-and-potato soup for Jill, pork sausage with warm potato salad for me — we were both pretty hungry. After lunch we strolled around the park and watched a group of businessmen playing *boules,* the French version of boccie. They had taken off their jackets and rolled up their sleeves and were in the middle of a game. They were quite good at it and the competition was intense. We sat in the early spring sun and watched for hours. We got to know these men; each one had a particular style, a personal approach to the game. Pierre was methodical, always repeating the same ritual before each shot; Jean-Paul was completely instinctual, laughing, relaxing himself before he threw. They seemed as if they were from another time, a Renoir time, when men were simpler and relationships between them less fraught with fear and distrust. They were very physical, putting their arms around each other, hugging, playfully hitting — as unselfconscious as boys.

It was now after four and we strolled over to the Left Bank to find the street market on the rue Buci that we had passed a few days before. We got turned around in the maze of little streets and never did find the market that day, but found ourselves in front of a gallery instead. In the window were delightful paintings, very colorful and audacious. We walked on, looking at other windows of other galleries, but kept going back to that window. Then a young man came out of the gallery and asked in English if we liked the paintings. We said we did — very much.

"I am the painter!" he announced proudly.

It turned out he was Dutch and had showed at this gallery before. We went in and looked at everything he had there, and at photographs of other work that was back in Holland. We chose a wonderful painting — a nude with a whimsical smile sitting on a divan in front of a window filled with stars. It hangs today in our entrance foyer; it's the first thing you see when you come into our house.

That night we started out walking — with no particular destination in mind. We strolled up to the Opéra and came across a huge boulevard filled with movie houses. We picked one and went in. It was an American movie that we hadn't been that interested in seeing back home, but with French subtitles it seemed so much more sophisticated. We bought popcorn, of course — but it had a caramel coating on it, sort of like Cracker Jacks. Well, the French don't know everything.

Afterward we strolled down the boulevard, which kept changing names — from the boulevard de la Madeleine to the boulevard des Capucines to the boulevard des Italiens. When it became the Italian one, we stopped and had a pizza, sitting outside, watching the people go by. If we closed our eyes for just a second, we felt like real people — not tourists. We were Parisians out for a movie and a pizza, and soon we would stroll home in the soft rain and go to bed. It felt like our town.

EIGHTEEN

New England

It has been said that the road has its own ending, and that the ending may have little in common with what you had in mind when you first set out. This karmic truth perfectly describes a weekend I recently spent visiting my son in camp.

He was in Vermont — the very center of Vermont — so we decided to fly to Boston, rent a car, and drive up. Then I had a brainstorm. I called our old friend Nora Pepper, who lives near Providence, and told her that we'd block out an extra day and drive down to visit her if she could get us all a dinner reservation. I wanted to go to Al Forno, which is a restaurant owned by Johanne Killeen and George Germon in Providence. I've been dying to eat there ever since I first started to cook from their wonderful cookbook *Cucina Simpatica*, which I have been staining, page by page, for the last few years. Their style of cooking could be called innovative, I guess, but that word usually makes me run in the other direction. I'm suspicious when innovation takes the place of inspiration and leads the artist to create something different just for its own sake. The word I would use for

their cooking is *emotional.* They have a way of making a dish en-
rich itself with its own flavors, rather than adding a lot of exotic
extras. A great example is their Rosemary Chicken. The bottom
layer is of sliced, roasted potatoes; then there's a layer of sliced
onions that have been sautéed in the same pan that the chicken
breasts were browned in. They lay the chicken on top with some
rosemary and tomatoes and roast everything in a very hot oven.
The roasting chicken releases its juices, which drip through the
onions onto the crisping potatoes — need I say more? These are
my people; they understand my soul — fat dripping through
onions onto potatoes. It was now time for us to meet in person.

Nora called back an hour later with the news that the restaurant was closed on Sundays. But I was too excited to let that
deter me.

"Call them personally and ask if they want me to cook for
them — at the restaurant or at home, whichever is more con-
venient."

Nora called back and said that they loved the idea, and let's
do it any other time, but that they would be in France that
weekend purchasing a house. For a moment I entertained the
idea of flying to France, but then I got hold of myself. This was,
after all, a weekend for visiting Max in camp. Glumly I made
plans with Nora to meet Sunday night in Boston at some restaurant or other, but in my heart I knew it wouldn't be the same.

The camp allowed us to visit Saturday from after breakfast
until after lunch and again on Sunday morning. Then they
wanted us out of there so that they could get things back to
normal. That gave us Saturday night on our own and most of the
day Sunday to drive back into Boston, where we would have
dinner with Nora, spend the night, and have most of the next
day to look around before flying home. I asked our travel agent
if there was a good place to eat in Vermont on Saturday and she

came up with an inn in the area that boasted "four-star gourmet" food. My hackles went up instantly. I had been burned before by a New England inn that used the word *gourmet*. That dinner had started with little plastic packages of saltines and steaming bowls of canned soup. Well, it was either canned or someone went to a lot of trouble to make it taste like canned. That was a "four-star" restaurant too. I want to know who's giving out all these stars. Michelin in France gives out three stars to only a handful of restaurants that they consider the best on the Continent, and here are places in rural New England where a meager three stars might go to a filling station that has a Coke machine. Maybe these places would be better off worrying more about their food and less about their stars. Anyway, Jill came up with a plan to save me from the "gourmet" inn and a potentially mediocre meal.

Ken Olin and Patti Wettig are friends of ours who have a house in Vermont. Jill called them up to see if they were going to be around. Ken's mom answered the phone and said that Ken and Patti were due in Vermont the following week and that it was Ken's birthday and why didn't we drop in and surprise him. She is a cookbook writer with a couple of wonderful books to her credit (written with Pino Luongo), and she promised a fantastic meal. Now wasn't this better than some stuffy old inn, said Jill, very proud of herself.

Our plans were solidly in place; but things started to go south just as we started to head north. We were to drive up from Big Sur, catch a plane in Monterey for San Francisco, then change planes for Boston. But our little puddle-jumper from Monterey was delayed at least two hours because of fog — June and July is fog time on the central coast — so there was no way we would make our connection in San Francisco. Jill ran to the other airline desks — Monterey's airport is really just one room — to find out if anyone else could get us there. Yes! U.S. Air had two seats on a plane leaving NOW. We grabbed our bags away from the United desk and sprinted for the plane. First problem solved. We were in plenty of time to make our connection. More time than we realized, it turned out. The flight to Boston was delayed three hours due to the same fog that moved in and out whimsically throughout the day.

This got us into Logan Field in Boston at midnight; by the time we rented a car and got our bags, it was almost one and we had a three-hour drive to Vermont ahead of us. But we were on West Coast time, so it was still early for us — no problem. An hour later it started to rain. Not normal rain, but an end-of-the-world kind of rain, the kind where your windshield wipers can't clear it off no matter how fast they're going. And we were the only people on the highway. That always gives me the creepy feeling that we're in a horror movie and we're the unsuspecting couple and everybody else but us knows that the axe murderer is waiting around the next bend in the road. Then we made a couple of wrong turns, which added just that little soupçon of tension between us to make the evening perfect. Or morning, I should say.

Our travel agent had talked us into renting a vacation house for the weekend rather than a room in a hotel or inn. This proved to be a bad choice. Since we were arriving after business hours, we had to find the main office of this resort community, where they had hidden our house key and directions. It was still pouring as Jill searched on her hands and knees for the cleverly concealed cubbyhole on the side of the porch. Finally she came up with the goods and we studied the directions by the map light in the car. We still had eight miles to go; it was now four in the morning and patience was running thin. The road got narrower and narrower and turned to dirt — or mud, I should say.

The car fish-tailed through the mud as we missed turn after turn. Fortunately, our bubbly sense of humor remained intact until we finally pulled up in front of the house.

The next morning came quickly. We had to get up early because Max would be waiting for us at camp and we didn't want to disappoint him. We put together a little breakfast from things we had bought at the 7-Eleven the night before and left, bleary-eyed, for camp.

Max was excited to see us, and we him. The day went beautifully. He showed us around, he introduced us to all his friends. The kitchen had prepared a little picnic basket for us, which we ate by the lake. We were thrilled with the camp. Then it rained — which was okay, because the camp director had promised that if it rained the parents could take their kids off the camp's grounds. Max couldn't have been happier. We found a McDonald's and ate a second lunch; we bought socks and underwear for Max, because all of his had disappeared; we had a ball. By the time we left camp for the day, Max had proclaimed it the best visiting day ever. He said it was perfect. We felt good. Tired, but good.

"Do we really want to go to Ken's party?"

"They're expecting us. We're the surprise."

"Yeah, but wouldn't it be better just to take potluck at that little inn? It's only a mile away from the house."

"It's too late now, honey. We can't call or we'll blow the surprise."

Their house was farther away than they had told us — a good forty-five minutes. And, of course, as soon as we headed out, it started to pour again. And I was low on gas; I suggested that we'd better stop on the way, but Jill was intent on not ruining the moment of surprise. This was where I should have taken over and insisted, but there's that weird, marital thing where you'd almost rather run out of gas so that later you can blame it on her. Maybe it's just my marriage, but I don't think so. It would be nice if they could invent a drug that fixed that.

We arrived at the Olins' at exactly the right time. We parked the car below so that they wouldn't see us coming. We crept up the hill in the mud and peeked through the window; there were Ken's parents and his two kids and another couple that turned out to be his sister and her husband. They were sitting at the dinner table eating what looked to be not exactly a festive meal. There was no Ken or Patti in sight. We poked our heads in and whispered, "Hello?" They looked at us as if we had lost our minds.

"Next week. The party is next week," said Ken's mom. There was one of those long pauses.

"No problem!" I said a bit too joyously. Jill eyed me from the side, a little worry line between her eyes.

In truth, I would have blamed it all on Jill in a second, but the way they all lined up behind Ken's mother and insisted that she couldn't possibly have made a mistake made me suspicious. They were obviously covering up — big time. So I hugged my honey and said "no problem" again, and asked if they knew where I could get some gas — real quick.

They told us to sit down. I really didn't want to. There might still be time to get back to that inn for dinner if we didn't run out of gas first, but they insisted. They had already cleared their plates and there obviously wasn't any food left, but they managed to find one piece of dry barbecued chicken that we could split. I really didn't want to eat that chicken. Jill looked over nervously once again. She knew that, for me, a bad dinner was worse than no dinner at all.

I yummed over the half piece of dry chicken, declined dessert, and said that we really had to find a gas station. They gave me directions: "Left out of our street, then the first right. That'll take you to the gas station by the highway." We thanked them hastily, laughed about our silly mistake, and beat it out of there. When I got to the bottom of the driveway, it started to rain again. Was there some cosmic connection between the rain and my car's ignition? When I started the car, God started the rain. Now, did they mean left out of the driveway, or left at the end of the street? He must mean the driveway. I turned left, then the first right, we drove for ten minutes and then the road turned to dirt — or mud, I should say. We had gone the wrong way. And we were on one of those dark roads that make me think of Hansel and Gretel — long way in, no way out. Now we would surely run out of gas. The adrenaline kicked in; Jill started that deep breathing she does when she's meditating. We were fucked.

I turned the car around and headed the other way. The needle was below the line and the light was blinking furiously. We got back to where we had made the wrong turn and figured that now we were heading in the right direction. We were. We passed through the little town that we were supposed to pass through, and then, in the rain, made another wrong turn. We caught this one quickly and doubled back to the little town and Jill ran into a restaurant to get directions.

"Just go up here to the stop sign and make a right. Then it's only three miles to the gas station." She jumped into the car and we were off. We drove almost five miles but couldn't find a stop sign.

"Where did she say the stop sign was?"

"She just said it was up here."

We doubled back to the restaurant. The gas light was now calling me names, blinking out "asshole" and "numbskull" on the dashboard in little red lights. Jill came out again.

"We were right; it's just a little farther."

And it was. And we found the gas station. And it was open. They had a little convenience store at the gas station, so Jill bought an apple and I bought some popcorn; I had noticed our house had a microwave. That was dinner.

The next morning at camp was no picnic. Max was sullen and didn't want to look at us. What happened is fairly classic — the first day is all about hello! and the second day is all about good-bye. Suddenly we're all facing four more weeks of separation — hard enough for the parents, but even tougher for the child who doesn't want his mates to see how upset he is. Maxie cried a bit and said that he was sorry it had to end this way, and we assured him that it wasn't the end and that it only meant that we loved each other a lot.

We decided it would be best if we got on our way immediately, and we were standing around trying to cope with it all when the camp director walked over with another couple in pretty much the same situation. They had a daughter who was throwing them out of camp. We talked for a bit and the husband reminded me that we had met years ago in New York. I had done a voice-over job for him. I asked him what he was doing now and he said that he was producing Julia Child's show on PBS. An electric tingle shot up my spine. I had a sense of destiny, of kismet. I have always loved Julia; I felt she was my spiritual mother, my mentor, although we'd never met. I explained this all to him.

"Well, if you're ever in Boston, I'm sure she'd love to meet you."

"I'll be in Boston tomorrow. All day." I really can be a pushy son of a bitch when a good meal might be forthcoming. But he was game and gave me his card. He said they would be prepping a show all day Monday in Julia's kitchen and that I should call sometime after noon. We said good-bye to each other and to our kids and got into our cars and headed for Boston.

We checked into the Ritz-Carlton, which has to be one of the best hotels in the world. They just know how to do it — without overdoing it. The travel agent had insisted we stay there and had thereby redeemed herself for that vacation-house fiasco in Vermont. We met Nora and a friend of hers for dinner at a place called Hamersly's, which turned out to be a delightful surprise — a wild mushroom sandwich, a poussin stuffed with prosciutto and other goodies, a brilliant roasted fish; the restaurant exceeded all expectations.

The next morning I took a walk down Commonwealth Avenue and found a good coffee shop. I read the paper while Jill was doing her exercises in the room. Then we hopped a cab for Harvard, where we explored the Fogg Museum, which was a treat. But I kept sneaking a look at my watch. Soon I would be able to call Julia. At exactly 12:30 I called her number and Geoffrey — my new friend from the previous day — picked up the phone.

"Come on over; she's dying to meet you — although I don't think she watches much TV other than *Murder, She Wrote.*"

He gave us directions and it turned out to be only a few blocks away. We walked through the campus, then through some lovely Cambridge streets until we reached hers. The numbers were hard to read, but there was a postman doing his thing, so I asked him where this address was.

"Oh, you're going to Julia's!" And he pointed it out.

The production crew was all over the house preparing for the next day's shoot of "Master Chefs in Julia's Kitchen" or something like that. The chef was in the kitchen weighing and measuring so that the recipes would be exact for the TV audience. We were introduced.

"You were in my restaurant last night," said Gordon Hamersly, a delightful young man who has become one of America's best restaurateurs and chefs. Once again that tingle of destiny crept up the back of my neck. Now, if one of these young production assistants would come in with a bluefish that she had caught yesterday and ask if we would all cook it together with Julia . . .

"I have this great bluefish I caught yesterday," said one of the young production assistants. "Why don't you guys do something with it for lunch?"

Then Julia appeared. She had been upstairs working on her computer. She welcomed us. We embraced warmly. And then with a wave of her hand, preparations were under way for lunch. Gordon was in charge — and he was brilliant. Julia looked on, adding bon mots where necessary; I peeled and seeded the tomatoes; even Jill pitched in. She knew that I was truly in heaven and she wanted to be there with me: cooking with a master chef and my revered Julia, in her kitchen, making tomato vinaigrette. What could be better?

Julia speared a piece of fresh mozzarella and put it together with a piece of tomato and a little arugula and popped it in her mouth. We were just standing around the kitchen work counter, eating and cooking. Someone opened a bottle of Chardonnay. Julia eyed the fish that Gordon was about to broil.

"I just read somewhere that the whole theory of rigor mortis in fish is undergoing a basic reexamination."

I looked up from my chopping — those famous dulcet tones, that wonderful look of earnestness peeking from under her bangs — was she seriously going to hold forth on fish rigor mortis? She was.

"It used to be "the fresher, the better." But now they're thinking it might be best to let the fish go *through* rigor mortis and come out the other *end* before you *cook* it. The texture is much better. Of course this is all still a theory."

"Who does this . . . fish rigor mortis testing?"

"Oh, there's all sorts of people that do all sorts of things."

I looked to see if she was having me on. But it's very hard to tell with Julia. She's very sly. At the same time her eye is twinkling with fun, it has a certain sternness to it that says, "Now don't you laugh at this, this is very serious," and then it twinkles again. And then she looks at you, very proud of herself, as if to say, "There. I'll bet you have no idea whether I was serious or not."

"How much money did they pay you on *L.A. Law*?" she asked — very directly.

"Oh, we were paid quite well. Especially in the last few years."

"Yes, but how much — per episode?"

And I told her. The question was asked so directly that I didn't even consider not answering. She nodded and filed the information away. I had the feeling it might come up in her next salary negotiation.

There was no dining room table, as the whole house had been taken over by the TV crew. So we set up at a card table with a plastic cover over it and dug into our wonderful feast — fresh-grilled bluefish with a tomato-herb vinaigrette, sautéed garden vegetables — it was all wonderful. Julia sat next to me.

"You see how this fish is a little mushy," she said, still onto the rigor mortis question. She pronounced it as if it rhymed with "pushy." I nodded. Anything she said was okay with me. Gordon, who had prepared the perfectly cooked fish, was across the table sitting next to Jill. He leaned close to her so as not to be overheard by Julia and muttered into his plate, "It's *not* mushy."

Gordon Hamersley was kind enough to send me his recipe for that delightful lunch:

Broiled Maine Bluefish with Tomato and Coriander Vinaigrette

Serves 13 to 15

For the bluefish

1 (8-pound) bluefish, skinned, pin bones removed, and cut into 7-ounce portions.

freshly ground pepper
zest of 1 lemon
salt

For the tomato vinaigrette

4 tomatoes, peeled, seeded, and chopped

2 teaspoons salt

2 shallots, peeled and minced

1 teaspoon chopped garlic sautéed in 1 tablespoon olive oil

1 / 2 bunch coriander, washed, dried, and roughly chopped

6 tablespoons olive oil

3 tablespoons red wine vinegar

For the vegetables

1 zucchini, cut into large rounds

8 potatoes, cut in half

8 small carrots, peeled and cut into rounds

olive oil

salt and freshly ground pepper

Special equipment
1 sheet pan, 1 pot for blanching vegetables, various bowls for making the tomatoes.

For the bluefish
Oil the sheet pan and place the fish fillets on it. Sprinkle them with pepper and lemon zest. Let rest in the fridge until ready to cook.

For the vinaigrette
Place the tomatoes in a colander and sprinkle with the salt and let drain for at least 1 / 2 hour. In a bowl combine the shallots, garlic, and coriander and reserve.

When the tomatoes have drained, add them to the bowl with the shallot mixture and then add the olive oil and vinegar.

For the vegetables
Bring 6 cups of water to a boil and blanch each of the vegetables until they are tender. Place them in a bowl together and toss with olive oil, salt, and pepper.

Preheat the oven at broil for 10 minutes. Salt the fish lightly and place the bluefish under the broiler for about 7 to 10 minutes, or until the fish is done.

To serve
Place the tomato vinaigrette on a serving platter and arrange the bluefish on top. Serve the vegetables separately in a serving bowl along with some cut lemons.

NINETEEN

Big Sur

🍇

↪ We colored eggs the night before. I say we, but it was
really just them: Jill and Max — mother and son, having a nurturing, creative, multicultural experience while Dad looked on.
Actually, I was cooking, nurturing a little in my own, solitary
way. I was throwing together a little garlic shrimp, known in
fancier circles as scampi, with a little pasta marinara on the
side. Serve this with a simple green salad (which Jill puts together — I hate to make salad).

The shrimp dish is simple to make and dazzling to serve. I
stole it from a little no-name roadhouse restaurant outside of
New Haven, Connecticut, when I was working at the Long
Wharf Theater in the midsixties. Shell, devein, and butterfly
some jumbo shrimp — maybe six to a person if they're actually
jumbo, more if they're only quasi-jumbo — finely chop six or
so cloves of garlic, and have ready some fresh, unflavored bread
crumbs, half a glass of white wine, and some chopped parsley.

Heat two tablespoons each of butter and olive oil in a large
skillet. When it's fairly hot, throw in the shrimp. Keep shaking

the pan to keep them from sticking too much. When they begin to turn opaque, throw in the garlic. Keep shaking the pan — you have to work quickly with this dish; you don't want the garlic to burn or the shrimp to cook a moment too long or they will get as rubbery as tires. Just when you think the shrimp is ready, tip a half glass of white wine in and let it sizzle and deglaze the pan for a moment. Before the wine is all evaporated, sprinkle a handful of the bread crumbs over everything and gently coat all the ingredients. The bread crumbs should soak up the oil, butter, and wine and adhere to the shrimp. Then turn the shrimp out onto a platter, add a little salt, throw on the chopped parsley, and serve with maybe a lemon wedge or two on the side. Try it; you can't miss.

It would have been nice to be a part of it — the Easter egg thing. Blowing goo out through little pinpricks in the raw eggs — don't inhale — and then dipping them into Paas Easter egg coloring and sticking on decals. But, alas, this kind of innocent, intimate family fun is a danger area for me. I always find myself backing away from it, automatically assuming I'll be no good at it. I don't know why; I'd probably be perfectly wonderful at egg blowing if I gave myself half a chance, but these things make me nervous. I love that it's happening; I heartily approve; it's just outside my area.

I think of my dad as I cook. Although my dad never cooked a day in his life, except for barbecues. Which, it suddenly occurs to me, is the only kind of cooking I'm no good at. I inevitably ruin barbecues. Food for thought. When I picture my dad, he's my age or thereabouts — just south of fifty. He only managed to live into his early sixties. I'm thinking as I stir the marinara, he wasn't all that comfortable being a father, either. He wasn't that comfortable doing anything. Not around the house, anyway. He had a little facial gesture — a nervous biting of the right side of his lower lip. It was very subtle, but I picked it up. To a son, a gesture like that is about as subtle as a train wreck. He worried the inner part of his lip by gently pulling it between his teeth and hesitantly gnawing at it while a line deepened between his eyes. The same line that's between my eyes.

Henry the ninth. He was the ninth of fifteen kids. My aunt wrote a book about the family and the only reference to my father was an anecdote about how they called him Henry the Ninth. Out of his whole life, that was all she could come up with. The other kids had stories, marriages, adventures, personalities — not my dad. Not in that book. He grew up in the middle of fifteen kids; his father died early on. Maybe that's why he was so nervous — in terms of parenting, I mean. He had no frame of reference. And then he passed it on to me. I may be one in a long line of shaky fathers — who knows, all the way back to Lithuania there's a whole genetic string of guys biting their lower lips and feeling nervous about coloring Easter eggs with their sons.

The week before, I had taken Max to work with me and he watched me entertaining the troops between takes. I was really on my game that night, showing off for my son a little. The next morning he chided me about it, but I could see he was really proud. "That's like me in class," he said. I know; the teachers have all told us what a pain in the ass he can be with the jokes.

He watches me. He sees me being funny, being naughty, garnering love and approval. Then he goes out and tests the waters. Is this being a man? How far can I go? Am I like my dad? Am I different? Am I better? That's the delicate question. You want to be better than your dad, and you don't. It's exhilarating and scary at the same time. I know I felt better than my dad. My mom made sure of that.

I watch them coloring the eggs. I stir the sauce. I look at my son's bright eyes, his perfect smile. And I think there are worse fathers in the world than I.

The next day was Easter Sunday and it was a beauty. This was our first springtime in Big Sur and it came after a winter that gave us fifty-two inches of rain. The green on the mountains was so green it was purple in some places. Big Sur has a way of taking the piney smell from the redwoods, cedars, and Monterey pines and stirring it together with the strong, salty ozone aroma of the ocean. Add a teaspoon or two of breeze from a crystal-clear morning and it stirs up a heady brew.

We had finished building our house the summer before, after three years of planning and seeking approvals from the myriad government agencies that protect Big Sur from people like us. We needed clearance from geologists, botanists, anthropologists (to scout for signs of Esselen Indian habitation), local architectural committees, and the daunting Coastal Commission, which forbids any development within sight of the beaches or Route 1. Since we were eager to comply with all regulations, we sailed through the process — albeit on a very slow boat — and began to understand and appreciate the way Big Sur inhales time, holds it deep in its lungs for what seems an eternity, and then blows it out as something completely different. Time stumbles out confused, diffused, and completely in its place. There are spaces between the ticks of the clock in Big Sur. Sometimes they're infinitesimal, noticed only by small dogs, but sometimes a grown person can fall into one and disappear for hours.

Our house sits on a ridge seemingly suspended between the Santa Lucia Mountains to the northeast and the Pacific to the southwest. Between us and the ocean is Pear Valley, which lies below us, and beyond that, Clear Ridge, which is about five hundred feet lower in elevation than we are and blocks our view of

Pfeiffer Beach — or, more appropriately, protects Pfeiffer Beach from having to see us. The floor of the valley meanders pretty much north to south, winding around Middle Ridge and Clear Ridge and then eking its way out to the sea. From above we can follow the line of the creek, canopied by a daisy chain of sycamores, that travels along the valley floor. It's called Bear Killed Two Calves Creek — dry in the summer months but rushing along at a pretty pace during the green time. I learned not long ago that it was named not by some early Native American inhabitant of the region but more probably by some blown-out hippie in the sixties. Great name though.

Ours is thought of as the "traditional" house on the ridge. It's a two-story log house with porches all around to catch the views. A friend described it as an East Coast, West Coast, Colorado house, and that about sums it up. It brings the outside in when the weather's nice and protects you from it when it's not. With lots of fireplaces and stone and wood and art collected from our friends or from our travels, the house is easy with itself, and easy on us. The center of the house is the kitchen, both architecturally and spiritually. I designed it with a lot of help both professional and amateur, and it is the kitchen of my dreams. Along with the standard gas stove — six burners, two ovens — there's a wood-burning indoor grill and next to it a wood-burning oven, for pizza, bread, cassoulet, and the like. It's a kitchen that can comfortably accommodate four to six people working together, but it's not too big for just me working alone. I tend to cook complicated things there, or things that take a lot of time, because I want to be there. When I'm away, I dream about it.

On Easter Sunday morning, it's pancakes and bacon on the griddle, fresh-squeezed juice, and strong coffee. And after, a trip to feed the horses, who live a mile up the ridge in their own beautiful place. Later we're invited to an Easter egg hunt and picnic at the Morganraths, so I want to spend the morning feeding, brushing, and then riding Tico, a chestnut gelding that I've been bonding with for the last few years. I ask Max if he wants to go with me.

"Can I drive?" he asks.

There's a feigned nonchalance in his delivery, but his eleven-year-old face gives him away completely. His tiny, pugnacious eyebrows challenge me.

"What's so weird about that?" they seem to say. "I know how to *drive,* for God's sake!"

His eyes are clear and innocent under those brows. So hot trying to be cool. I pause for a second, caught short by this sudden, bold foray into the swamp of father-son relationships.

"Sure," I say.

And I feel a little surge of parental achievement. I know that in that short pause lived a hundred noes, a hundred reasons for turning him down. But something — perhaps the directness of his challenge, perhaps the rare request for intimacy, perhaps the singular freshness of the morning — moved me to say yes. And why not? What am I afraid of? Maybe it's race memory. I remember the palpable fear in my father's eyes whenever he was left alone with me. He looked like a lion tamer eyeing a particularly dangerous beast. "This is my job," his eyes seemed to say, "and I have no idea how to do it."

"You can get it out of the driveway," says Max.

I ease the unwieldy Suburban out of the narrow driveway and face it up the dirt road toward the horse meadow. It's about a mile of twisty, narrow, virtually untraveled road and poses no danger whatsoever — other than a drop-off on the left that would plunge you hundreds of feet into the valley below. On the right are overhanging trees that lower the resale value of your car fifty bucks a scrape. I move the seat back so that my toes can barely reach the gas peddle and tilt the wheel up so that he can fit onto my lap. I drop into the lowest gear and we start — slowly, tentatively — up the road of life.

"Don't tell him anything," I think. "He can do it himself."

Max is locked in concentration. The big truck doesn't steer easily and he tends to oversteer into every turn.

"Whoa!" he says out loud.

There we are, the boy and his father, both feeling proud of ourselves, both inwardly celebrating the boy's moment of independence — or, more correctly, nondependence.

But there is an unspoken communication between us, deeper and stronger and surer than the obvious, greeting-card, rite-of-passage celebration. The boy, sitting on his father's lap, surrounded by his power and experience and love, thinks: "Don't help me, but be there. Let me have the freedom, let me fantasize the power, but be there. Not to show me, not to guide me. Just be there."

Later that day, after the picnic, after the sun had gone down, in another context long forgotten, he asked, "When you're fifty, that means you're halfway through, right?" "Right," I said, easily, quickly. Another lie, perhaps the sweetest one, but another lie — in a day full of sweet lies.

The picnic is a yearly event held at the Morganrath compound, about a mile down the ridge from us. Helen is the matriarch of the clan and the force behind not only the Easter celebration but also Christmas candle-dipping and various other pagan rituals that gather the denizens of Pfeiffer Ridge. She is helped by her children — two boys, Helmuth and Jali, and two girls, Celia and Tara — all married, all with children, and all living on the ridge. The boys have never left; the girls did, and returned, husbands in tow, to start and raise their families.

There's no pigeonhole I can think of to fit these people into — not aging hippies; they're more rooted, more connected to place and family. But they're not indigenous either, not grown from local soil — more like a family of migrating mountain goats that grazed onto the ridge, caught a whiff of something different, and stayed on. They sensed that all the things that seemed serious and important and ponderous elsewhere break up in this tangible atmosphere; they fragment, turn to dust, and blow up the coast to Monterey.

We arrived with our colored eggs and our potluck pasta salad and introduced ourselves to everyone, because we're the new kids on the block. Helen orchestrated the food so that the day was a kind of rolling banquet. She designated some people to bring breakfast items — sweet rolls, frittatas, sausages, bacon biscuits, and the like — and that rolled slowly into brunch, with more substantial egg dishes, Steve Pappas's Greek Easter bread, a little champagne sneaking into the orange juice. She's a believer in constant food flow, and she plays her dining room table like a Stradivarius. Brunch becomes lunch — a more serious event, with maple-glazed hams, turkeys, pastas (our humble salad was inhaled in seconds), and the best deviled eggs I can remember. Then, as if by magic, the bones were gone and dessert was spread before us like a confectioner's window display. Pecan pie, ollalaberry pies, chocolate cake — the best — homemade ice creams, sugar cookies, and on and on and on.

The party flowed with less force and direction than did the food. People talked in small groups, the kids mixed and played. The men for the most part talked with the men, and I joined in conversation when I could. There was a spirited debate about whether to pave the blessedly unpassable road that was bumped over by all the residents of the ridge. The traditionalists yelled at the futurists; the environmentalists yelled at both of them. It was hard to believe that such energy and vehemence could be summoned over such a dusty, bumpy little road. But it was *our* bumpy road, damn it! And nobody was going to force me to pour concrete on it . . . ; I just nodded and agreed with everybody. I was new.

The formal events began later in the afternoon. First there was a play. It was directed and adapted by Helen's daughter Tara and acted by all the grandkids of the family and a few friends from the neighborhood. It was called Tiki, Tiki, Tembo and based on an old Chinese story. The kids had made masks and costumes, and Tara narrated with great gusto.

Then all the kids were herded inside while the adults hid every sort of Easter egg you could imagine — hundreds of them all over the huge compound; in the trees, in grown-ups' pockets, at the bottom of the pool, under uncles' hats. Then the kids were let loose, with the understanding that if a little kid could find it, the older kids would let it alone. There were enough for everyone.

The older children, ages eight to thirteen or fourteen, willingly suspended their adulthood for this moment. They let themselves forget their dignity and their seriousness and their raging hormones so that they could wear masks, roll on the lawn, act like old Chinese characters, hunt for eggs, be children in the eyes of their parents, until Easter Sunday passed and they had to return to the drudgery of growing up.

But the parents, too, could suspend time and be parents in the old, Norman Rockwell sense of the word — watching their children, swapping recipes, recalling their youth, disparaging their kids to each other with such unabashed pride and love that they didn't even try to hide it.

I watched my son watching these children. What was he thinking? I'll never really know. But I could see his mind working, a nervous swallowing gesture as he placed himself — his life — in relation to the rest of these children in their momentary idyll. And I watched me watching him. It was as if a part of me had disengaged from my body and was suspended above the ridge, looking down on this Renoir-painted scene with its colors blending out of focus at the edges. What was it about these people that moved me so deeply? I barely knew them. They seemed nice enough; their values were similar to mine; they worked hard and loved their children and respected their neighbors. All well and good. Why did I find myself desperately trying to swallow a hot lump in my throat? These people I didn't know from Adam had unloosed a yearning in me, a longing for a place in my childhood that I had never had: the innocent time, the time when I didn't have to be on guard. It never was. This simple, serendipitous picnic, this easygoing, unconstructed, ordinary event that was allowed to take its own shape, that wasn't controlled or manipulated, was not from my world; it never had been. No bargaining; no negotiating for love; no offering of warmth, only to pull it away as in the hand-slapping game of Flinch, to send you spinning into uncertainty, never knowing who would be there to catch you.

When I was eleven or so, we had a Passover seder at my Uncle Buster's house. My mother and her sisters sealed themselves in the kitchen for two days before the event to make gefilte fish — and like that eastern European version of pike quenelles, the sisters, raw with familial memories and sibling jealousies, were pushed together into tight little balls of hysteria and set into the pressure cooker of each other's company. Whenever I passed the vile-smelling kitchen, I saw their angry faces with tight-set mouths and yellow, dragon eyes darting furiously at each other. They barely spoke, the steam bubbling out of their ears. Or so it seemed. We were gearing up for Passover.

The Passover service and dinner started with false calm. Everyone smiled and said nice things to each other, but we all knew that the house was filled with tension and animosity. My mother and her sisters had by now regressed to eight years old and were vying for the attention and approval of their father, who had died many years before. Uncle Buster — my father's brother and my favorite uncle, puckish and kind and ready to please — began the service as he had done every year with the Hebrew prayers sung sweetly in his husky tenor, his eyes sparkling with irony at the mock seriousness of his tone. We children loved it.

"The children don't understand, Buster. Do it in English," said my mother. "It's important they understand."

"I will. I will," he said. "Don't worry." And his voice rose again in lilting cadences and trills and descended in minor tones that sounded almost like weeping.

My mother's mouth tightened and she started to nod as if only she understood. Her eyes narrowed.

"I worry," she said. "I'm the only one who does." This was pronounced darkly, a subtle rebuke to her sisters, perhaps. Buster smiled and continued the prayer, hoping the moment had passed. But we all knew it hadn't.

Suddenly my mother pushed her chair back violently and rushed into the kitchen. Immediately my Aunt Margie, Uncle Buster's wife, followed her to soothe her, to take her side as she always did.

"Buster," she pleaded over her shoulder as she went to the kitchen, "Do it the way she says. Please."

Buster laughed. He didn't care; he would do it standing on his head, for all he cared. My father and the other uncles got into it now, laughing with Buster, their hero. "Sing it in English, Bus!" "Show her what it sounds like!" And we all started to joke and sing the stilted English translations in the old Jewish melodies. No one realized the violence of the storm brewing in the next room.

We had progressed to just before the Four Questions, where the youngest child would ask the traditional questions that would summon forth the explanation of why we celebrated Passover, when suddenly my mother sprang from the kitchen. Tears were leaping out of her eyes. She was screaming at Uncle Buster — I can't remember the words. He tried to placate her, to calm her. My father, too. But everything made her angrier. Her face looked so hurt — as if Buster, my father, all of us, the world, was pointing an accusing finger at her, belittling her, mocking her. Finally Buster could take no more. He stopped trying to soothe her and began screaming back, using words like *crazy* and *madwoman*. That fanned the flames even hotter. He threw the prayer book down in disgust and left the room; he left the house — his own house — started the car, and was gone. Margie was crying, almost keening, "It's nothing, it's over nothing!"

In all the chaos, I was aware only of my brother and myself, sitting very still, looking at the table, ashamed. We were like statues, stiff and cold. She was ours. No one else's mother went crazy; no one else's mother hated Uncle Buster and drove him from his own house.

Everyone left. My mother off into the night to God knows where; my father off to find her. Other aunts and uncles wrapped the uneaten food to take it home for another day. My brother, who was older, went off to find friends. He pretended to be cool, but I know he hurt like I did.

I think this is why I cook. Not because I love food, which I do, passionately, but to finish that meal, once and for all. To finish that meal with grace and calm and convivial family conversation, with laughter and warmth. Mostly, I think about warmth; so that I can melt away the cold of that uneaten dinner.

Perhaps these things skip a generation. I'm doomed to shun Passover seders no matter how much work I do with my therapist, no matter how many friends tell me that I'm missing something really wonderful. But maybe my son will be curious. Maybe he'll want to seek out the buried traditions of his dad's religious background. Maybe he'll complete that seder with his family, teaching his children the story of the Jews coming out of Egypt. And his son will ask the Four Questions and he'll warm with pride and satisfaction at passing on an ancient and wonderful tradition. I like to think that's how these things work out.

Ollalieberry Pie with Custard Topping
Serves 8

I'd like to end the book with a dessert recipe, and this Big Sur classic will suit just perfectly. I got it from Alix-Ann Loveland, who caretakes our house up there; she got it from Linda Van Allen, who lives down the ridge aways. Linda won't tell who she got it from.

Ollalieberries are a cross between a loganberry and a youngberry and look like a reddish blackberry. Although I'm told they also grow in Oregon, the only ones I've ever seen are around the central coast of California. Their season is short — about five weeks around June and early July. If you can't find them, substitute blackberries, or even a combination of blackberries and raspberries.

The crust

1 cup unbleached all-purpose flour	4 tablespoons unsalted butter
1/4 cup sugar	1 1/3 tablespoon lard
1/4 teaspoon ground cinnamon	1 tablespoon freshly squeezed lemon juice
pinch of salt	

Filling

1 quart ollalieberries (or blackberries as a substitute)	1 tablespoon lemon juice
3/4 cup sugar	3 tablespoons flour

Custard topping

3 eggs, well beaten	1 cup sour cream
1/2 cup sugar	8 ounces cream cheese

Prepare the crust: Mix the flour, sugar, cinnamon, and salt in the bowl of a food processor fitted with the steel blade. While it's running, add the butter and lard until it forms a coarse meal. Then add the lemon juice and process briefly until it forms into a mass. Wrap it in plastic wrap and chill for a half hour.

Preheat oven to 400°.

In the meantime, gently mix the filling ingredients in a bowl. Let the mixture sit at room temperature.

Roll out the chilled dough on a lightly floured surface to form a circle slightly larger than a nine-inch pie tin. Transfer the dough to the pie tin and press it into the bottom and sides. It should have a little extra around the sides. Fold that back toward the inside and crimp it. This will help to hold the filling.

Place a sheet of aluminum foil, shiny side down, onto the dough, weight it down with some pie weights, and bake the pastry for fifteen minutes.

Remove the crust from the oven; remove the foil and weights; fill the crust with the berry filling.

Put the beaten eggs and sugar in a small saucepan and cook over low heat, stirring until mixture begins to thicken. Then add the sour cream and the cream cheese and keep stirring until it's smooth.

Spread the custard over the pie and bake for ten minutes.

Then lower the oven to 350°, and bake 30 to 40 minutes until the custard begins to brown.